CHARCUTERIE BO

COOKBOOK

150+ GORGEOUS AND MOUTHWATERING PLATTER RECIPES | HOW TO PAIR CHEESES, MEATS, CRACKERS, FRUITS, AND NUTS TO CREATE THE ULTIMATE BOARD

Table of Contents

Introduction   5

Chapter 1: The Ingredients of the Board   2

The Pairing Art   2

The Lead Actors   3

The Supporting Cast   3

Behind the Scenes   3

Bringing it All Together   4

Types Of Charcuteries   4

Salt-Cured   5

Smoke-Cured   5

Air-Cured   5

Brine-Cured   5

Confit   6

Forcemeat   6

Regional Styles   6

Chapter 2: Morning Boards   8

Classic Gingerbread Gentlemen   8

Brandied Christmas Cut-Outs   9

Snow Ball Cookies   10

Holiday Spice Cutout Cookies   11

Traditional Christmas Sugar Cookie   13

Butter Christmas Cookies   15

Kiss Sugar Cookies   16

Austrian Vanillekipferl Christmas Cookies   17

Fruitcake Cookies   19

Glazed Italian Christmas Cookies   20

Christmassy Hedgehog Slices   22

Christmas Tree Meringue Cookies   23

Peppermint Chocolate Chip Cookies   25

Chapter 3: Afternoon Boards   26

Jamón Experience   26

Kids in Bologna   27

Salami Keto Lovers   28

Summer Berry Fields   29

Cherries and Almonds   31

Afternoon for Two   32

Sweet Belgium   33

South of France   34

The Sicilian Table   35

Happy Hour Tapas   36

Sour Then Sweet   38

Chapter 4: Evening Boards   40

Beef Noodle Egg Rolls   40

Mushrooms and Beef Egg Roll   41

Beef and Caramelized Scallion Fried Dumplings   42

Cheese and Beef Chips   43

Cheeseburger Dip   44

Ground Beef Canapés 45

Beef Patty Lettuce Wraps 46

Runza 46

Sage Venison Sausage 48

Sweet Italian Venison Sausage 49

Summer Sausage 50

Soy Sauce Stewed Eggs 51

Teriyaki Pork Tenderloin 52

Cha Shu Pork 53

Tamagoyaki Japanese Omelet 54

Tokushima Ramen 55

Country Casserole 56

Wakayama Ramen 57

Sapporo Miso Ramen 58

Hiyashi Chuka Cold Ramen 60

Okinawa Soba 62

Homemade Tonkotsu Ramen 64

Tonkotsu Miso Ramen 65

Creamy Tonkotsu Ramen 66

Tonkotsu Toridashi Ramen 68

Tonkotsu Shio Ramen 70

Yummy Pork Noodle Casserole 71

Fast Miso Ramen 72

Instant Pot Tonkotsu Ramen 73

Singapore Noodles 74

Asian Crab and Cucumber Salad 75

Chilli Prawn Noodles 75

Suckling Pig, Jellyfish, and Noodle Salad 76

Singapore Bee Hoon 77

Chilli Prawn Noodles 78

Seafood Shio ramen 79

Katsu Curry Ramen 80

Long–Life Noodles 82

Shrimp Garlic Ramen 83

Instant Pot Curry Ramen 84

Shrimp Gyoza 85

Beef and Orange Stir Fry 86

Chili Beef with Broccoli, Egg, Noodles, and Oyster Sauce 87

Beef, Noodle, and Noodle Stir Fry 88

German Spaghettini 89

Chapter 5: Anytime Boards **90**

Chunky Chili-con-Carne 90

Hungry Man Stew 92

Pioneer Goulash 93

Beef Chili 94

Classic Beef Chili 95

Beef Cheesy Chili 96

Slow Cooker Simple Cheesy Chili Recipe 97

Garlic and Spice Beef Chili 98

Mom's Chili 99

Classic Chili Con Carne 101

Chili Con Carne I 102

Chili Con Carne II 103

Hakata Tonkotsu Ramen 104

Tokyo Ramen 106

Thai Shrimp Noodle Soup 108

Cranberry Nectarine Salad 109

Kurume Ramen 110

Tsukemen Ramen 111

Kitakata Ramen 113

Sesame Noodles 114

Noodles with Butter 115

Salmon Miso Ramen 116

Fast Miso Ramen 117

Asian Shrimp and Noodle Soup 118

Dad's Favorite Casserole 119

Beef and Water Spinach Noodles 120

Chapter 6: Special Occasion Boards **121**

Cheesy Ground Beef Salad 121

Deep-Fried Prawn and Rice Croquettes 122

Marvel's Japanese Fried Oysters (Kaki Fuh Rai) With Lemony Tartar Sauce 124

Orange Ponzu 125

Baby Spinach and Ground Beef Salad 126

Cesar Ground Beef Salad 127

Creamy Almond and Ground Beef Salad 128

Bacon Cheeseburger Balls 129

Enchilada Meatballs 130

Bacon Cheeseburger Dip 131

Sweet Ketchup and Bacon Meatloaf 132

Hamburger Broccoli Dip 133

Family Style Meatloaf with Tomato Gravy 134

Southwestern Classic 135

Big John's Oyster Motoyaki 136

Broiled Mochi with Nori Seaweed 137

Cream Cheese and Crab Sushi Rolls 138

Chapter 7: Preserves, Spreads, Dips, and Condiments **139**

Moroccan Mezze 139

Spanish Seaboard 141

Golden Celebration 143

Easy Butterscotch Sauce 144

Hot Fudge Sauce 145

Rum and Butter Sauce 146

Vanilla Cream Sauce 147

Pineapple Ginger Sauce 148

Fireball Whisky Sauce 149

An Italian Date 150

A Night In 151

Chapter 8: Nuts, Olives, and Pickles **153**

Baked French Brie with Peaches, Pecans, and Honey 153

Cauliflower Pecan Florets 154

Cream of Walnut Soup 155

Feta, Roasted Red Pepper, and Pine Nut Pancakes 156

Macadamia Nut Hummus 157

Pistachio-Crusted Shrimp with Orange Zest 158

Spanish Almond Soup 159

Squash and Pecan Flatbread with Ricotta and Dried Cranberries 160

Tomato, Raisin, and Pine Nut Bruschetta 161

Tropical Chicken Salad 162

Almond Crusted Cheesy Grapes 163

Cheddar-Pecan Crisps 164

Curried Tropical Nut Mix 165

Feta-Nut Fritters 166

Macadamia Nut Caramel Popcorn 167

Pine Nut and Zucchini Fritters 168

Roasted Almonds with Paprika and Orange 169

Slow Cooker Candied Nuts 170

Honey Mustard Nut Mix 171

Candied Pecans 172

Old South Pralines 173

Smoky-Sweet Almonds 174

Maple Rosemary Nuts 175

Chocolate Raisin Clusters 176

Chocolate Peanut Clusters 177

Fruit and Nut White Clusters 178

Swedish Nuts 179

Trail Mix with Dark Chocolate and Toasted Coconut 180

Baked Cod with Walnuts 181

Cashew Nut and Pesto Pasta 182

Cashew, Spinach, and Cannellini Bean Stew 183

Chargrilled Lamb Cutlets with Macadamia Pesto 184

Creamy Cashew Curry 185

Conclusion **187**

Introduction

What do we mean when we say "charcuterie"? In its truest form, it refers to meat—usually pork—that has been preserved by salt-curing, smoking, air-curing, or brine-curing

Aside from being a great way to showcase and enjoy the incredible array of smoked, salted, and cured meats from the world of charcuterie, they are a perfect conversation starter and gathering place for guests. It has become so central to our get-togethers that we also include them in our chef business. When we prepare for events and celebrations, we always bring a charcuterie board to break the ice and get the conversation going. There is comfort and connection created when sharing thoughts and feelings over food.

While charcuterie is a French word, people across many cultures have been preserving meat for centuries. It was once a necessity to keep this precious commodity for a long time without spoiling, long before the invention of the refrigerator. This ancient style of preserving meats by drying and salting extended the life of meat during the heat of summer and kept it safe to eat over a long, cold winter.

We believe in bringing people together over a memorable meal. It's a tradition in our home to gather every Sunday with family and friends, and one of the most important offerings we produce is a beautiful charcuterie board. The ritual is a natural extension of our Italian and Spanish heritages, with parents and grandparents who taught us about ingredients and flavors common on antipasto and tapas plates.

Through this guide, you will learn how to make incredible charcuterie arrangements that will get your guests talking. There are 30 themed arrangements, ranging from small to large, for just about any occasion. We've also shared 32 of our recipes for accompaniments—such as dips, condiments, bread, pickles, jams, spreads, and other bites—to bring extra homemade flavors to your boards

Chapter 1: The Ingredients of the Board

- **Meat:** For a charcuterie lover, this will be the star of the show. It's worth it to splurge on high-quality meats. If you're catering to a larger group, choose two or more types.
- **Cheese:** While there are hundreds of cheeses, a good basic rule is to choose two or more with different flavor profiles and textures. Choose one cow milk cheese, which can be soft or hard, and either a sheep or goat cheese, which are typically sharp and softer cheeses. That way you have something for everyone.
- **Produce:** Fresh fruit like berries, grapes, and cherries look beautiful and bring balance to a plate. There is also all manner of dried, pickled, and brined items, such as gherkins and olives, to round things out. Nuts, such as pistachios, almonds, and hazelnuts, bring some welcome crunch.
- **Dips and condiments:** These are finishing touches in terms of flavor profile and appearance. Your options include dips, jams, relishes, honey, mustards, and chutneys.
- **Bread and crackers:** These are the platforms on which to consume your charcuterie. They present a great opportunity to explore the specialty baked goods of regional cuisines and your local bakery. If you're preparing a spread for friends who can't eat gluten, then crackers made from rice, lentil, quinoa, and seeds are great choices.

The Pairing Art

Now comes the most creative part of the process: the art of the arrangement. Generally, you'll want to incorporate each of the five key elements of a board to create a harmony of colors, textures, and flavors.

The Lead Actors

The first thing to consider is which charcuterie will take center stage. Once you know this, you can select the next most important component, the cheese. When the charcuterie and cheese are eaten together, consider how they will create balance and each enhance the flavor of the others. For example, if you've picked some rich and salty meat such as prosciutto or jamón, some creamy cheese like a nutty gruyère or milky mozzarella will provide equilibrium. If you've chosen a heavier, more seasoned meat like salami, go for a fresh and silky burrata or even a sharp cheddar as an interesting counterpoint.

The Supporting Cast

Once you have chosen the meat and cheese, the rest should start to fall into place. What fresh produce will brighten up the board and provide a contrast for the richness of the meats and cheeses? Dried fruits like apricots offer extra sweetness, and pickled foods like cornichons bring sweet and sour notes to round out the flavor profile. Brined items like olives offer a salty, tangy edge. And nuts are especially useful to include a contrasting texture on the board.

Dips and condiments help put the finishing touches on your board. Consider what flavor profile needs to be added. Need a light touch? Perhaps some ricotta or a hummus dip would work. Looking to bring extra acidity and bite? Some tangy mustard can elevate the flavors of your meats and cheeses. Want a sweet or sour touch? Jams and preserves can offset salty and savory flavors.

Behind the Scenes

You'll need some basic tools in your kitchen to bring together your charcuterie boards. Start with a cutting board. We prefer wood because it's easier on your knives. You'll need some kitchen knives for the cutting and slicing that goes on behind the scenes. You'll also need a tool for shaving harder cheeses. You can buy a fancy cheese shaver or just use a wide vegetable peeler.

We suggest a few small and medium bowls for mixing ingredients. You'll also need a kitchen scale to measure the ingredients listed in the boards in chapters 3, 4, and 5. Get a small, inexpensive digital scale. You should be able to find one online for under $20.

Bringing it All Together

Let's say your friends who are traveling to Paris soon are coming over for Sunday brunch. It's winter and you know you want to do a French theme. You could create a spread of jambon de Bayonne (or its Italian cousin, prosciutto), gruyère, croissants, freshly squeezed orange juice, espresso, sweet pastries, and marmalade.

Because it's winter, toasting the croissants with the meat and cheese stuffed inside couldn't be more warming. The chewy prosciutto, gooey melted cheese, and crisp toasted croissant offer an array of textures.

The delicate, salty flavor of the prosciutto pairs perfectly with gruyère, a sharp yet creamy cheese that melts well. Oranges are readily available in the winter, so freshly squeezing the juice is easy, and this sweet, tart, acidic touch serves as a palate cleanser. All of those flavors are

sure to create a culinary experience. If you want to take it a step further, make your own Meyer Lemon Marmalade for a balance of tart and sweet.

As you can see, on this board we have paired different flavors and textures. There is something salty, sweet, sour, and buttery, with a variety of savory notes, together with sweet and acidic tones to offset the savory. It's important to include all of them on each board.

Types Of Charcuteries

While specialty meats and fish were once found only in artisanal stores in North America, a newfound interest in charcuterie has meant that supermarkets and local grocery stores are increasingly offering a greater variety of options that go well beyond old-school cold cuts.

These days you can find all manner of charcuterie, including both traditional varieties and more modern types with creative flavorings. Broadly speaking, though, charcuterie falls into a handful of categories related to the method of preservation.

Salt-Cured

The method of salt-curing meat is very simple—all it takes is salt, air, and time. Salt gradually draws moisture out of the meat, making it difficult for bacteria to survive and so producing a more shelf-stable product with a pleasingly salty flavor. This basic method of preservation is often combined with other forms, such as smoking, drying, and brining, to add flavor and texture.

Common types: bacon, lox, Parma ham, prosciutto.

Smoke-Cured

An ancient preservation method, smoke-curing involves exposing meat and fish to smoke, but without fully cooking it. It is commonly done by placing the food in an enclosed area over smoke produced at low heat from smoldering wood or charcoal for a long period. This can also be done with cold smoke that cools when pulled into a separate chamber from where the product is held.

The smoke provides a coating on the surface of the product that prevents the growth of bacteria and aids in dehydration, yielding tender and distinctly flavored foods. The depth of flavor can be further enhanced by changing the variety of wood. Apple and pecan woods are a couple of our favorites that add beautifully sweet notes.

Common types: smoked ham, smoked salmon, smoked sausages.

Air-Cured

Drying meat by gently circulating air is another popular method of preservation. The most commonly recognized air-cured meat is salami, which is flavored with aromatics such as pepper, garlic, and wine, then placed in casings to be hung in a temperature-controlled cellar for an extended period. Air-curing is also a key part of the cheese-making process.

Common types: biltong, jamón, jerky, salami.

Brine-Cured

Essentially an extension of basic salt-curing, this method of preservation involves submerging products in a brining solution of liquid and salt. The liquid can be water, beer, cider, fruit juice, or wine, flavored with aromatics such as pepper, citrus, herbs, and spices such as anise and cloves. This form of curing allows products to absorb extra seasoning while also preserving them with salt.

Common types: brined ham, brined pork belly, pastrami.

Confit

Confit involves a combination of salt and animal fat. The meat is first dry-salted and then immersed in its own rendered fat at a low temperature for a long period. It is most commonly done with duck, and we even show you how to make your own for our South of France board. A life-changing variation is a confit rib eye clarified in tallow.

Common types: duck confit, goose confit, pork belly confit.

Forcemeat

The softer side of charcuterie, forcemeats are pureed mixtures of meats, poultry, or fish combined with fats and seasoning to preserve and flavor the products. While these can be an acquired taste for some, the most common type on a charcuterie board is undoubtedly liver pâté, a rich, smooth delicacy that makes for a

wonderful spread on a humble baguette. You can try it out on our Picnic in Paris board.

Common types: mousse, pâté, rillette, terrine.

Regional Styles

While different cuisines around the globe have their own variations on preserving meat, the true home of charcuterie is Europe, where it is a highly regional and seasonal affair, incorporating local ingredients at the peak of their freshness.

- **France:** The French are pioneers in charcuterie, where preserved meats are common in homes, restaurants, and wine bars across the country. They are masters of dry-curing to create delicacies such as jambon de Bayonne and saucisson sec, and experts in forcemeat products such as pâtés, mousses, and terrines.

- **Italy:** If you have ever been to Italy, you know it's common to see all kinds of small-batch salami hanging from the rafters in local shops and homes. They're just one type of an array of cured meats, known collectively as salumi and

6

typically made from pork, to grace antipasto platters across the nation.

- **Spain:** Pork reigns supreme as the charcuterie item of choice on tapas plates in Spain. The most prized is Jamon ibérico, which is artfully salt- and air-cured from heritage pigs. Also popular is chorizo, a cured or smoked pork sausage that is seasoned with garlic, paprika, and salt, among other variations.

- **Eastern Europe:** Often overlooked when it comes to charcuterie, Eastern Europe has its own traditions of salting and smoking meats. In Poland, you can savor smoked or dried kielbasa, and in Hungary, you'll find various types of salami and cured kolbász (sausage).

Chapter 2: Morning Boards

Classic Gingerbread Gentlemen

Preparation time:	Cooking time:	Servings:
10 minutes	40 minutes	3

Ingredients

- ⅓ cup butter or butter flavored shortening
- ½ cup dark molasses
- ¼ cup dark brown sugar
- ¼ cup white sugar
- 1 egg
- 2 cups flour
- 1 ½ teaspoon baking powder
- 2 teaspoons ground ginger
- 1 teaspoon cinnamon
- ½ teaspoon salt

Directions

In a bowl combine the butter or butter-flavored shortening, molasses, brown sugar, and white sugar. Using an electric mixer, blend until creamy.

Add in the eggs and continue beating until blended.

In another bowl, sift together the flour, baking powder, ginger, cinnamon, and salt.

Working in increments, slowly add the dry ingredients into the wet ingredients, mixing just until blended.

Cover the dough and place it in the refrigerator for at least one hour or until firm.

Remove the dough from the refrigerator and preheat the oven to 375°F. Lightly grease or line a baking sheet.

Roll the dough out onto a lightly floured, flat surface.

Use gingerbread men cutouts that measure approximately 6 inches tall to cut out the shapes of the cookies.

Transfer the cookies to the prepared baking sheet and place it in the oven.

Bake for 10-12 minutes, or until the edges are nicely browned.

Cool on a baking rack and frost, if desired.

Note: If desired, you can decorate your gingerbread gentlemen with nuts or candies before baking.

Brandied Christmas Cut-Outs

Preparation time:	Cooking time:	Servings:
10 minutes	40 minutes	3

Ingredients

- 1 cup butter, softened
- 1 ½ cup sugar
- 2 eggs
- 1 tablespoon plus 2 teaspoons good quality brandy
- 1 teaspoon pure vanilla extract
- 3 cups flour
- ½ cup pecans, finely ground
- ½ teaspoon cinnamon
- ½ teaspoon ground ginger
- ½ teaspoon nutmeg
- ¼ teaspoon salt

Directions

In a large bowl, combine the butter and sugar. Using an electric mixer, blend the ingredients until creamy.

Next, add the eggs, brandy, and vanilla extract and mix until blended.

In a separate bowl, sift together the flour, cinnamon, ginger, nutmeg, salt, and finely ground pecans.

Working in increments, add the dry ingredients into the wet and mix until blended.

Cover the dough tightly with plastic wrap and place the dough in the refrigerator for at least 2 hours or overnight.

Remove the dough from the refrigerator and preheat the oven to 400°F.

Lightly dust a countertop with flour and roll the dough out into approximately ¼ inch thickness.

Using your choice of cookie cutters, cut the cookies out into circles or festive shapes and then place them on an ungreased cookie sheet.

Place the cookie sheet in the oven and bake for 10-12 minutes, or until golden brown.

Snow Ball Cookies

Preparation time:	Cooking time:	Servings:
10 minutes	40 minutes	5

Ingredients

- 2 cups pecans
- 1 cup butter, at room temperature
- 1¼ cup powdered sugar, and more if required
- 2 cups all-purpose flour

Directions

Preheat the oven to 300°F, and place the oven rack in the middle position.

Place the pecans in a food processor. Pulse until the nuts are all crushed finely.

In a mixing bowl, add the butter and ¼ cup of the powdered sugar. Beat on high until creamy, about 2 minutes.

Add the pecans to the butter mixture. Beat on low speed until just combined.

Add the flour gradually, and beat until well mixed.

You should get a thick batter.

Make about 48 balls of even size about ¾" to 1" in diameter. Take the time needed to roll well with the palms of your hands.

Place the balls on an ungreased cookie sheet, about ½" apart.

Place in the oven, and bake for 40 minutes.

Place the remaining powdered sugar in a shallow dish.

Roll the balls in the powdered sugar, while they are still hot but cooled enough to handle. Place on a waxed paper to rest.

Repeat a second time, rolling the snowball in the powdered sugar. Add some powdered sugar if needed.

Cool completely before placing in an airtight container, and refrigerate.

Holiday Spice Cutout Cookies

Preparation time:	Cooking time:	Servings:
10 minutes	10 minutes	3

Ingredients

- Dough
- ¼ cup unsalted butter (softened)
- ¾ cup sugar
- ¼ cup apple sauce
- ¾ cup molasses
- 1 egg
- 3 tablespoons fat-free milk
- 3¾ cups all-purpose flour
- 1 teaspoon ground ginger
- 2 teaspoons ground cinnamon
- 1 teaspoon ground aniseed
- 1 teaspoon ground cloves
- 1 teaspoon baking soda
- Frosting
- ¼ cup unsalted butter (softened)
- 5 cups confectioners' sugar
- ½ teaspoon pure vanilla extract
- 4 to 5 tablespoons milk
- Colored sugar crystal or sprinkles, for decoration, if desired

Directions

In the large mixing bowl of the electric mixer, cream the butter and sugar until pale yellow and fluffy.

Beat the apple sauce, molasses, egg, and milk for about 2 minutes.

Stir together the flour, cinnamon, ginger, aniseed, cloves, and baking soda in a mixing bowl. Mix well.

Add the dry ingredients to the creamed mixture. Beat until you obtain a smooth dough. Cut in 2, and cover each dough half with plastic wrap. Refrigerate for at least 2 hours until the dough is firm.

While the dough is resting in the refrigerator, prepare the frosting. Beat the butter and sugar with an electric mixer set on high speed until light and creamy. Beat in vanilla and enough milk to achieve a light and fluffy consistency.

If you want colored frosting, separate the frosting in a little plastic container and add a tiny bit of food coloring of your chosen color. Mix well. Add more food coloring if required to have the color you want. Again, I use food coloring paste as the colors are more vivid and it takes so little.

Cover the frosting in airtight containers until ready to use.

Lightly sprinkle some flour on a clean working surface. Using a rolling pin, roll out one of the cookie dough halves to ¼". Keep the second half of the dough in the refrigerator until you are ready to use it.

Cut the cookies out with Christmas-shaped cookie cutters.

If the cookies are to be used as decorations for the Christmas tree, make a hole using a plastic straw, set at least ¼" inch from the edge of the cookie top.

Place 1" apart on ungreased baking sheets lined with parchment paper. Bake at 375°F for 8-10 minutes or until the edges are golden brown. Remove from the oven, and let the cookies cool down completely before frosting.

Traditional Christmas Sugar Cookie

Preparation time:	Cooking time:	Servings:
10 minutes	40 minutes	4

Ingredients

- Dough
- 1 ½ cups powdered sugar
- 1 cup butter, softened
- 1 teaspoon vanilla
- 1 egg
- 2½ cups all-purpose flour
- 1 teaspoon baking soda
- 1 teaspoon cream of tartar
- Frosting
- 2 cups powdered sugar
- ½ teaspoon vanilla
- 2 tablespoons milk or half-and-half
- Food coloring, if desired
- Colored sugar crystal or sprinkles, if desired

Directions

With an electric mixer set on medium, mix powdered sugar, butter, vanilla, and egg in a large mixing bowl until well blended.

Add flour, baking soda, and cream of tartar. Mix until the dough becomes smooth, about 3-4 minutes.

Divide the dough into 2 balls, and wrap them in plastic wrap. Refrigerate for 3 hours or more, until the dough is firm.

While the cookie dough is resting, prepare the frosting. In a medium bowl, beat all frosting ingredients until smooth and fluffy on high speed for about 3-4 minutes.

If you want colored frosting, separate the frosting into little plastic containers, and add a tiny bit of food coloring of your chosen color. Mix well. Add more food coloring if required to have the color you want. I use food coloring paste as the colors are more vivid, and it takes so little.

Cover the frosting in airtight containers until ready to use.

Preheat the oven to 375°F and place the oven rack in the middle position.

Lightly sprinkle some flour on a clean working surface. Using a rolling pin, roll out one of the cookie doughs to ¼". Keep the second half of the dough in the refrigerator until you are ready to use it.

Cut the cookies out with Christmas-shaped cookie cutters.

If the cookies are to be used as decorations for the Christmas tree, make a hole using a plastic straw, set at least ¼" inch from the edge of the cookie top.

Transfer the cookies to an ungreased cookie sheet lined with parchment paper.

Place in the oven and bake for 7 to 8 minutes or until light brown. Remove from the oven, and let the cookies cool down completely before frosting, about 30 minutes.

To frost the cookies, stir each frosting color with a spoon or small whisk until smooth. Place in a small plastic bag. Cut off a small piece of the bag's corner. Push out the frosting onto the cookie slowly. Frost and decorate cookies as desired with frosting and colored sugars.

Butter Christmas Cookies

Preparation time:	Cooking time:	Servings:
10 minutes	40 minutes	3

Ingredients

- 1 cup butter, softened
- 3 ounces cream cheese, at room temperature
- ¾ cup white sugar
- 1 large egg
- 1 teaspoon pure vanilla extract
- 3 cups all-purpose flour
- Colored sugar crystal for decoration, red, green, and multicolored.

Directions

In a mixing bowl, beat the butter and cream cheese with an electric mixer on high speed until light and fluffy, about 2 minutes. Add the sugar. When well mixed, put in the egg and vanilla. Beat until well mixed on medium speed, about 2 minutes.

Gradually add the flour by increments of half a cup. Beat at about medium speed until well combined and a ball of dough forms, about 4 minutes.

Split the dough in two. Wrap each half with plastic wrap.

Put in the refrigerator for about 2 hours or until the dough is firm.

Preheat the oven to 375°F and place the oven rack in the middle position.

Take one of the dough halves out of the refrigerator, and keep the other half in the refrigerator until you are ready to use it.

Lightly sprinkle some flour on a working surface. With a rolling pin, roll out the dough to about ¼" thick.

Using various Christmas-shaped cookie cutters, cut out the shapes.

Transfer the cookies to ungreased cookie sheets lined with parchment paper, leaving 1" between each cookie.

Sprinkle the cookies with red, green, or multi-colored sugars before baking.

Place in the oven, and bake for 7-9 minutes or until the edges are lightly golden brown. Remove from the oven.

Sprinkle the cookies with more colored crystal sugar while the cookies are still warm.

Kiss Sugar Cookies

Preparation time:	Cooking time:	Servings:
10 minutes	40 minutes	3

Ingredients

- 48 chocolate Kisses, of the flavor of your choice, I like peppermint for the holidays
- ½ cup butter, at room temperature
- 1 cup white sugar
- 1 large egg
- 1½ teaspoons vanilla extract
- 2 cups all-purpose flour
- ¼ teaspoon baking soda
- ¼ teaspoon salt
- 2 tablespoons milk
- Red or green sugar crystals

Directions

Preheat the oven to 350°F and place the oven rack in the middle position.

Unwrap the chocolate kisses and set them aside.

With an electric mixer, cream the butter and sugar on high speed until fluffy, about 2-3 minutes.

Add the sugar, vanilla, and egg, and beat until well mixed.

Combine flour, baking soda, and salt. Stir until well mixed.

Add gradually the flour mix with the butter mixture. Add the milk. Beat until the cookie dough is light and smooth.

Place colored sugar crystals in a shallow dish.

Form 1" balls with the palm of your hands. Drop the formed cookie balls in the colored sugar and cover it with the sugar.

Place the prepared cookie on an ungreased cookie sheet lined with parchment paper.

Bake for 8 to 10 minutes or till the edges of the cookies become golden brown.

Remove from the oven. Let cool for a few minutes.

Place a candy in the middle of each cookie.

Place the cookies on a wire rack with a spatula. Allow to cool down completely, about 20-30 minutes.

Austrian Vanillekipferl Christmas Cookies

Preparation time:	Cooking time:	Servings:
10 minutes	40 minutes	3

Ingredients

- 1 vanilla bean
- 14 tablespoons (1¾ sticks) unsalted butter
- 2 cups all-purpose flour
- ½ cup white sugar
- 1 cup almond meal
- 3 egg yolks
- ½ teaspoon baking powder
- 1 pinch salt
- Powdered sugar

Directions

Split the vanilla bean lengthwise, and scrape the inside of the bean with a knife. Set aside.

In the large mixing bowl of the electric mixer, cream the butter, vanilla bean scrape, and white sugar on high speed until light and fluffy.

Add the almond meal, and beat until well mixed on medium speed.

Add the egg yolks, and beat until well mixed.

Combine the flour, baking soda, and salt in another mixing bowl. Stir well.

Add the dry ingredients to the creamed mixture. Beat on low speed until all the ingredients are just combined, and you have a smooth dough.

Split the dough into 4 pieces. Form a long roll shape with each of the 4 pieces of dough. Wrap in plastic wrap, and refrigerate for 2 hours until the dough is firm and very cold.

Preheat the oven to 350°F, and place the oven rack in the middle position.

Cut pieces from the dough to form a cylinder of about ½" in diameter and 2½" in length. Make the extremities thinner and give the cookies a quarter-moon shape.

Place the cookies on an ungreased cookie sheet lined with parchment paper.

Bake for about 12 minutes, until the cookies' edges are becoming slightly golden.

Remove from the oven, and place the cookie sheet on a wire rack to cool down.

Place some powdered sugar in a shallow dish. When you can handle the cookies with your hand, roll the cookies in the powdered sugar twice.

Once they have completely cooled down, place the cookies in an airtight container. They will keep for up to a week...but they won't last that long!

Fruitcake Cookies

Preparation time: Cooking time: Servings:

10 minutes   40 minutes   7

Ingredients

- 1 cup butter, softened
- 1 cup powdered sugar
- 1 egg
- 1 teaspoon pure vanilla extract
- 1 tablespoon bourbon
- 2 ¼ cup flour, sifted
- ¼ cup candied ginger, chopped
- 1 cup pecans, chopped
- 1 ½ cup dried or candied fruit assortment (cherries, pineapple, apricots, etc), chopped

Directions

Using an electric mixer, combine the softened butter and powdered sugar until creamy.

Add in the egg, vanilla extract, and bourbon. Continue mixing until blended.

Working in increments, add in the sifted flour just until blended.

Add the pecans, candied ginger, and dried or candied fruit to the bowl. Using a spoon, mix until the nuts and fruits are worked in evenly throughout the dough.

Cover the dough with plastic wrap and place in the refrigerator for 1 hour.

Remove the dough from the refrigerator and divide it into three equal sections.

Roll each section into a log and wrap it securely with plastic wrap. Place the logs back into the refrigerator for at least two hours or overnight.

Remove the cookie logs from the refrigerator and preheat the oven to 325°F.

Unwrap the logs and slice the dough into pieces that are approximately ¼ inch thick.

Place the cookies on an ungreased baking sheet, making sure to leave at least ½ to 1 inch between them.

Place the cookie sheet in the oven and bake for 12-15 minutes, or until the cookies turn a light golden brown and the edges begin to crisp.

Glazed Italian Christmas Cookies

Preparation time:	Cooking time:	Servings:
10 minutes	30 minutes	3

Ingredients

- ½ cup butter
- 2 cups white sugar
- 4 large eggs
- 3 tablespoons baking powder
- 2 tablespoons pure vanilla extract
- 2 tablespoons pure almond extract
- 4 cups flour
- Frosting
- 2 cup icing sugar
- ½ cup milk
- 1 teaspoon almond pure extract
- Food coloring, if desired
- Sugar sprinkle for decoration, if desired

Directions

With an electric mixer, cream the butter and the sugar until smooth.

Add the eggs one by one, beating at medium speed.

Add the baking powder and vanilla and almond extract.

Gradually add the flour one cup at a time. Mix until you have a ball of firm dough.

Split the dough in two, and form two balls. Wrap in plastic wrap, and chill dough in the refrigerator for 2 hours.

Preheat the oven to 375°F, and place the oven rack in the middle position.

Place one of the dough balls on a lightly floured surface. Roll out the dough to ¼" thick. Cut the cookies out using Christmas-shaped cookie cutters. Keep the second dough ball in the refrigerator until you are ready to use it.

Place the cutout cookies on ungreased cookie sheets lined with parchment paper.

Place in the preheated oven, and bake for 8-10 minutes, until the edges of the cookies start to brown.

Remove from the oven, and let the cookies rest for 10 minutes before placing them on a wire rack. Let cool down completely before glazing them.

While the cookies are cooling down, you can prepare the glaze. In a small bowl, place the icing sugar. Add the almond extract and just enough milk to make a nice frosting consistency.

To glaze, dip the top of the cooled-down cookies into the glaze. Decorate with pearls or colored sugar or sprinkles.

Let dry completely before serving.

Christmassy Hedgehog Slices

Preparation time:	Cooking time:	Servings:
10 minutes	60 minutes	8

Ingredients

- ½ cup butter
- 1 8 ounce/250 g package shortbread cookies such as Scotch finger biscuits
- 1 teaspoon vanilla extract
- ⅔ cup white sugar
- ½ cup dry cranberries
- ½ cup pecans or almonds
- ½ cup tablespoons coconut flakes
- 2 tablespoons baking cocoa
- 1 cup semi-sweet chocolate chips
- 1 can of sweetened condensed milk (14 ounces/300 g)
- Cooking spray

Directions

Line the bottom of an 8" round cake pan with wax paper or parchment paper. Grease the pan side and paper liner bottom with cooking spray.

In a saucepan, over medium heat, melt the chocolate chips with the condensed milk and butter, about 4-5 minutes, stirring occasionally with a wooden spoon. Remove from the heat, and let it cool down for a few minutes.

Crumble the cookies in small pieces, about the size of hazelnuts or peas, in a large mixing bowl.

Add the coconut, pecans, cranberries, and cocoa. Stir a few times to combine.

Pour the chocolate mixture into the mixing bowl with the dry ingredients. Stir until all the ingredients are well coated.

Christmas Tree Meringue Cookies

Preparation time:	Cooking time:	Servings:
10 minutes	40 minutes	3

Ingredients

- 4 large egg whites
- 1⅓ cups superfine sugar
- ¼ teaspoon cream of tartar
- ¼ teaspoon salt
- ¼ teaspoon peppermint extract (optional)
- Green food coloring (gel is preferred, and just a little is needed))
- Green gel writing frosting (optional)
- 1 ounce of semi-sweet chocolate (optional)
- Material
- Piping bag with a star fitting tip
- Cookie sheet lined with parchment paper
- Large clean cookie sheet for the chocolate star

Directions

Preheat the oven to 150°F, and place the oven rack in the middle position.

Beat the egg whites on high speed until foamy and white.

Add the cream of tartar, the salt, and the peppermint extract if desired. Continue beating at high speed until soft peaks form.

Add the sugar very, very slowly as the mixer continues to beat the egg white mixture at medium-low speed. It should take exactly 7 minutes. This step is important. It will make your meringue light and fluffy. It can be useful to set a timer so as not to lose track of the time you need to incorporate the sugar.

Add a few drops of green food coloring, and mix it in with a spatula or wooden spoon until you get the desired color shade.

Place the meringue mixture in a piping bag already set with a star-shaped tip.

Cut some parchment paper to fit the bottom of a large cookie sheet.

Pipe the meringue in a continuous movement to shape small Christmas trees with a pointing tip finish, about 1" apart from each other.

Bake for 2 hours to 2½ hours until the meringue cookies are dry and crispy.

Check often on the meringue cookies after 1¾ hours so they do not start to brown.

Remove from the oven. Let cool on a wire rack.

To make the chocolate star for the treetop, place a cookie sheet in the freezer for 10 to 15 minutes until it is very cold.

Reverse the cookie sheet on your working surface so the bottom is facing you.

Melt the chocolate in the microwave for about 30 seconds, until it's all melted but not burned. Let it cool down for about 2 minutes.

Place the melted chocolate in a fabric piping bag set with the smallest round tip.

Draw in one movement the star shape on the back of the cold cookie sheet. Make as many as you have meringue for.

Wait until the chocolate star is completely cooled down to remove them delicately with a spatula.

Carefully glue a star onto each meringue treetop with the green writing gel frosting. Add some gel frosting on the Christmas tree if desired to create shade.

Sprinkle it with powdered sugar to imitate snow.

Peppermint Chocolate Chip Cookies

Preparation time:	Cooking time:	Servings:
10 minutes	40 minutes	3

Ingredients

- 1 cup butter, softened
- 1 cup white sugar
- ½ cup light brown sugar
- 2 eggs
- 2 teaspoons peppermint extract
- 1 teaspoon pure vanilla extract
- 2 cups flour
- ½ cup dark cocoa powder
- 1 teaspoon baking soda
- 1 teaspoon baking powder
- ¼ teaspoon salt
- 1 cup white chocolate chips
- 1 cup crushed candy cane pieces

Directions

In a large bowl, combine the butter, white sugar, and brown sugar. Using an electric mixer, blend the ingredients until creamy.

Next, add in the eggs, peppermint extract, and vanilla extract and mix until blended.

In a separate bowl, sift together the flour, cocoa powder, baking soda, baking powder, and salt.

Working in increments, mix the dry ingredients into the wet ingredients.

Add the white chocolate chips and crushed candy cane pieces into the bowl and fold in until the chips are worked evenly throughout the dough.

Cover the dough with plastic wrap and refrigerate for at least 2 hours.

Remove the dough from the refrigerator and preheat the oven to 350°F.

Using your hands, form the dough into balls measuring approximately 1 inch in diameter.

Place the balls on an ungreased baking sheet and then place the baking sheet in the oven.

Bake for 10-12 minutes or until done.

Chapter 3: Afternoon Boards

Jamón Experience

Preparation time:	Cooking time:	Servings:
10 minutes	40 minutes	3

Ingredients

- 1 cup Castelvetrano olives (or any mild green olive), not pitted
- 6 ounces jamón ibérico (or prosciutto), thinly sliced
- 4 ounces Manchego (or any mild sheep milk cheese), broken into rough pieces
- 1 baguette
- 2 tablespoons garlic-infused olive oil
- Sea salt

Directions

Fill a small bowl with Castelvetrano olives and place it near the top right corner of the board.

Gently fold the jamón in wavy ribbons near the center top of the board.

Place the roughly broken pieces of Manchego below the jamón in the center of the board.

Tear the baguette in half. Leave one-half intact, and with a serrated knife slice open the other half.

Gently brush a small amount of olive oil inside the sliced baguette pieces, then sprinkle the oiled sides with sea salt. Brush one stroke of oil across the top of the uncut piece. Place the bread on the left side of the board.

Drink pairing: Manzanilla is a Spanish sherry best served chilled to accompany cured meat or seafood. It has a dry, fresh, and delicate palate of floral notes reminiscent of chamomile, almonds, and yeast. It's absolutely perfect with jamón and this tapas-style spread.

Kids in Bologna

Preparation time:	Cooking time:	Servings:
10 minutes	40 minutes	3

Ingredients

- 6 grissini sticks
- A small bundle of fresh basil leaves
- 2 tablespoons balsamic reduction or glaze
- 1 cup cherry tomatoes
- 8 ounces fresh Mozzarella bocconcini (or fresh mozzarella cut into bite-size pieces)
- 4 ounces mortadella (or any mild deli meat), thinly sliced

Directions

Place the grissini in a glass sticking straight up and barely offset from the center of the board.

At the base of the grissini glass, place the bundle of basil and a mini bowl of balsamic reduction.

Visually divide the board into thirds (imagine drawing a peace sign on the board), and place the cherry tomatoes, bocconcini, and mortadella each in its own section.

Drink pairing: Chocolate egg cream—a delicious and kid-friendly blend of chocolate syrup, milk, and seltzer—is a classic of Italian American soda shops in New York City. For each serving, blend ½ cup whole milk and ¼ cup chocolate syrup together. If you have an immersion blender or high-speed blender, you can get that frothy texture and soda shop experience. Pour the chocolate milk into a tall glass and top with seltzer. Finish with a cute straw and serve.

Pro tip: Chill the glasses in the freezer for a frosty cold treat.

Salami Keto Lovers

Preparation time:	Cooking time:	Servings:
10 minutes	45 minutes	2

Ingredients

- 1 cup fresh garlic ricotta (see Variation)
- 4 Mini Chaffles
- Extra-virgin olive oil, for drizzling
- Freshly ground black pepper
- 3 ounces Salami Picante, casing removed, thinly sliced
- 3 ounces Creminelli Whiskey Salami Minis (or any mild salami)
- You will also need: a board, a small bowl, a small spoon, a small upright dish or glass

Directions

Prepare the fresh garlic ricotta and chaffles according to the recipes. The ricotta can be prepared up to a week ahead of time, but the chaffles are best served warm or at room temperature.

Place the ricotta in a small bowl with a spoon, near the center of the board but slightly to the left. Drizzle it with olive oil and grind some pepper over the top.

Arrange the chaffles off to the right side of the ricotta, stacking and shingling them to look pretty.

Arrange the salami slices below the ricotta.

Put the mini salami sticks in a small upright dish or glass near the top left side of the board.

Drink pairing: Keeping with the keto theme, pair this spread with some replenishing electrolyte water. Packed with sodium, potassium, and magnesium, this is a must for keto dieters (who tend to lose electrolytes due to water loss) and a great pick-me-up for anybody who wants to feel hydrated and refreshed. In a pitcher, combine 3 cups of filtered water, ¼ teaspoon sea salt, 130 mg potassium powder, and 45 mg magnesium powder. Squeeze in the juice of half a lemon and stir well to mix.

Summer Berry Fields

Preparation time:	Cooking time:	Servings:
10 minutes	3 hours minutes	3

Ingredients

- 1 cup Oven-Dried Strawberries
- 4 ounces pancetta, thinly sliced
- 1 tablespoon olive oil
- 1 tablespoon granulated sugar
- 2 teaspoons lemon juice
- ½ cup blackberries
- 1 cup raspberries
- 4 thick slices of brioche
- 2 tablespoons unsalted butter
- Pinch ground cinnamon
- Pinch confectioners' sugar
- 8 ounces mascarpone cheese
- 2 tablespoons honey
- You will also need: a platter, a small bowl, a small spoon, a butter knife, a small jar, a honey wand

Directions

Prepare the oven-dried strawberries according to the recipe. The strawberries can be prepared up to 2 weeks ahead of time.

Heat a skillet over high heat. Add the pancetta and drizzle with the olive oil. Sauté the pancetta for 6 to 8 minutes, until it crisps up like cooked bacon. Set aside.

In a medium bowl, mix the granulated sugar and lemon juice. Add the blackberries and raspberries, and gently toss to coat them with the mixture. Set aside to steep for 5 minutes.

Toast the brioche slices and spread with the butter. Place the brioche along the left side of the board, from the top to just below the center. Top the brioche with the macerated raspberries and blackberries. Finish with a sprinkling of cinnamon and confectioners' sugar.

Spoon the mascarpone into a heap near the lower right corner of the brioche.

Place the crispy pancetta on the top right corner of the board.

Pile the oven-dried strawberries in a small bowl, and place it in the bottom left corner with a small serving spoon next to it.

Just above or next to the strawberries, place the honey in a small jar with a honey wand.

Drink pairing: Some French champagne is a great accompaniment to this board. If you are celebrating and want to splurge, Dom Pérignon is the ultimate pairing, but if you'd like to go with something lower-key but still elegant, fresh, and light, an authentic Brut such as Canard-Duchêne is great, too.

Cherries and Almonds

Preparation time:	Cooking time:	Servings:
10 minutes	45 minutes	3

Ingredients

- ½ cup Pecan Granola
- 2 cups plain Greek yogurt
- 4 ounces bresaola (or lonzino), thinly sliced
- 2 cups cherries
- 1 cup Marcona almonds (or any salted blanched almonds)
- 5 to 6 ounces honeycomb squares
- You will also need: a board, 2 small bowls, 2 spoons, a small knife

Directions

Prepare the pecan granola according to the recipe. The granola can be prepared up to a month ahead of time.

Divide the Greek yogurt into two small bowls and top each with half of the pecan granola. Set the bowls side by side in the center of a large board with a spoon in each bowl.

In the top right corner, arrange the bresaola.

In the bottom left corner, add the cherries.

Above the cherries, pile the Marcona almonds.

On the bottom right, add the honeycomb squares, with a small knife.

Drink pairing: The sweetness and textures of this board make an exciting pairing with kriek, a hoppy, cherry-flavored beer from Belgium typically made with sour cherries. American brewery Strange Craft Beer Company makes a great one, but for the real deal, try Belgium's Lindemans Brewery kriek lambic beer.

Afternoon for Two

Preparation time:	Cooking time:	Servings:
10 minutes	50 minutes	2

Ingredients

- ¼ cup Pancetta-Onion Jam
- 2 tablespoons Cabernet Balsamic Reduction
- 8 ounces burrata (or fresh mozzarella)
- 1 cup arugula
- Sea salt
- Freshly ground black pepper
- Extra-virgin olive oil
- 4 ounces Barolo salami (or any richly seasoned salami), thinly sliced
- 2 small loaves fougasse (or focaccia or ciabatta)
- You will also need: a board, a cheese knife, a small bowl, a small spoon

Directions

Prepare the pancetta-onion jam and cabernet balsamic reduction according to the recipes. The jam can be prepared up to 2 weeks ahead of time, and the reduction up to 3 months ahead of time.

Place the burrata in the center of a small board and top with the arugula, letting it naturally cascade around the cheese. Season with salt, pepper, and a drizzle of olive oil. Place the cheese knife next to the burrata.

Spoon the pancetta jam in the bottom left corner, near the base of the burrata.

Pour the cabernet balsamic reduction into a small bowl and place it in the right top corner with a small spoon in it.

Add the salami near the balsamic reduction in the right corner.

Cut the bread into small pieces and scatter them in the bottom right corner.

Drink pairing: Cabernet Sauvignon is a scrumptious and fruity full-bodied red wine that is a beautiful complement to the complex flavors of the Barolo salami, pancetta-onion jam, and balsamic reduction. Simply choose your favorite bottle and you cannot go wrong.

Sweet Belgium

Preparation time:	Cooking time:	Servings:
10 minutes	50 minutes	3

Ingredients

- 1 cup Date Caramel
- 5½ ounces chocolate salami (or dark chocolate)
- 5 ounces Fromage de Bruxelles (or any soft cow milk cheese, or double-cream brie)
- 4 hazelnut croissants (or plain croissants spread with Nutella)
- 4 plain croissants
- 1 cup raspberries
- 2 cups strawberries
- You will also need: a large board, a small knife, a small bowl, a small spoon, a cheese knife

Directions

Prepare the date caramel spread according to the recipe. If necessary, this can be made up to 3 days ahead of time, but it's best served fresh.

Slice half of the chocolate salami into thin rounds. Place the slices and the remaining large piece in the bottom right corner of the board. Put a small knife next to it.

In the center of the board, place the Fromage de Bruxelles with a cheese knife.

Put the date caramel spread in a small bowl with a spoon and place it in the top right corner of the board with a small spoon in the bowl.

Stack the croissants along the left side of the board.

Scatter the raspberries on the Fromage, cascading down one side.

Fill in the blank spaces around the date caramel bowl with the strawberries.

Drink pairing: An espresso martini is an invigorating drink to accompany this board. To make one, combine 2 ounces vodka (we like White Nights Vodka from Belgium), ½ ounce simple syrup, ½ ounce coffee liqueur, and 1 ounce chilled brewed espresso in a cocktail shaker filled with ice. Shake well, then strain into a martini glass garnished with a rim of chocolate sprinkles.

South of France

Preparation time:	Cooking time:	Servings:
10 minutes	20 minutes	3

Ingredients

- 12 ounces Duck Confit
- ½ cup Mustard Gastrique
- 8 ounces Fromage blanc (or quark)
- 2 ounces caviar
- 4 large hard-boiled eggs, diced small
- 1 small red onion, minced
- 6 ounces black pepper crackers
- You will also need: a large platter, 2 small bowls, a small serving fork, 2 small spoons, a small dish, a caviar spoon, 4 small teaspoons

Directions

Prepare the duck confit and mustard gastrique according to the recipes. The confit can be prepared up to 3 months ahead of time and reheated, and the gastrique can be prepared up to 2 weeks ahead of time and reheated. Put the warm duck confit in a small bowl with a serving fork, and place the bowl on the top left side of the board.

Place the Fromage blanc in a small bowl with a spoon on the bottom right side of the board.

Place the caviar in a small bowl in the center of the board, with the caviar spoon in it. Place the teaspoons beside it.

To the left of the caviar, place the diced hard-boiled eggs. Just above the eggs, place the minced red onion.

Below the caviar, spoon the warm mustard gastrique directly onto the board, then use the back of the spoon to pull it to the right, creating an artful look. Leave the spoon to the side.

Arrange the crackers in both the upper right and lower left quadrants.

Drink pairing: A delicate and fruity champagne will provide a crisp, refreshing contrast to the flavors of this board. We recommend Le Mesnil Blanc de Blancs Grand Cru, which has a subtle fruitiness perfumed with hints of apple and pear and is readily available online.

Ingredient tip: You can use whatever kind of caviar appeals to you. Unopened caviar can be stored in the refrigerator for about 2 weeks.

The Sicilian Table

Preparation time:

10 minutes

Cooking time:

40 minutes

Servings:

6

Ingredients

- 2 cups Rosemary-Lemon Castelvetrano Olives
- 1 Artisan Focaccia, cut into large squares
- 1 (4-ounce) log goat cheese
- ¼ cup chopped salted pistachios
- 5½ ounces salami with pistachios (or any flavorful salami), sliced
- 5½ ounces fennel salami (or any herb-infused salami), sliced
- You will also need: a large board, a small cheese knife, a medium bowl, a spoon

Directions

Prepare the rosemary-lemon olives and artisan focaccia according to the recipes. The olives can be prepared up to a week ahead of time, but the focaccia is best served warm or at room temperature.

Roll the log of goat cheese in the chopped pistachios. Place the log to the left-center of the board. Stick a small cheese knife on the top of it.

Place the pistachio salami slices in the left bottom corner of the board.

Place the fennel salami in the bottom right corner of the board.

Fill a medium bowl with the marinated olives, add a spoon, and place it in the top right area of the board.

Scatter the focaccia squares along the top of the board, reaching from side to side.

Drink pairing: Keeping with the theme, you can pair this board with some olive vermouth, the sister to the well-known dirty martini. It's a briny cocktail that will complement the citrus notes of the olives and the saltiness of the salami. In a tumbler, combine ⅔ ounce dry vermouth, ⅓ ounce fresh orange juice, 1 ounce of scotch whiskey, and a few ice cubes. Stir well for about 20 seconds. Strain into a cocktail glass and finish with 3 Castelvetrano olives on a stick. A mocktail version can be made with white grape juice in place of the vermouth and a splash of cream soda in place of the scotch.

Happy Hour Tapas

Preparation time:	Cooking time:	Servings:
10 minutes	50 minutes	4

Ingredients

For the chili oil Manchego

- 12 ounces Manchego (or any mild sheep milk cheese), cut into bite-size pieces
- 1 fresh chile, thinly sliced
- 1 cup extra-virgin olive oil
- For the crushed tomato crostini
- 1 baguette, sliced
- 1 garlic clove, cut in half
- Extra-virgin olive oil, for drizzling
- 1 large, ripe heirloom tomato

For the board

- ½ Spanish Tortilla
- 1 cup arugula
- Extra-virgin olive oil, for drizzling
- Freshly ground black pepper
- Sea salt
- 6 ounces salchichón ibérico (or any Spanish hard salami), sliced
- 6 ounces chorizo, sliced
- You will also need: a medium board, a jar with a cover, a small fork

Directions

To make the chili oil Manchego:

Put the Manchego pieces in a medium jar. Add the chile slices and pour in the olive oil, making sure the cheese is submerged.

Screw on the lid and set aside for at least 1 hour so the oil and peppers can infuse fully into the cheese.

To make the crushed tomato crostini:

Preheat the oven to 375°F.

Spread out the baguette slices on a rimmed baking sheet. Toast in the oven for 7 minutes.

Rub one side of each slice with a cut garlic clove and drizzle with olive oil.

In a food processor or blender, pulse the tomato until it resembles a coarse salsa.

To make the board:

Prepare the Spanish tortilla according to the recipe. The tortilla can be prepared the day before and reheated. Cut it into 1-by-2-inch rectangles and place the pieces in the center of the board. Top with the arugula, a drizzle of olive oil, and a few grinds of black pepper.

Place the crostini along the bottom of the board, from the center to the right side. Spoon the tomato puree over the crostini and season with sea salt and freshly ground black pepper.

Place the salchichón ibérico slices in the top right area of the board.

Place the chorizo slices in the bottom left corner of the board. Put a small fork in the jar of Manchego and place it in the top left.

Drink pairing: A young or aged Tempranillo, a full-bodied Spanish red wine, would be a great choice for this board. Depending on your preference, you could also go with a young, fruitier version or an aged, bold, high-tannin wine with hints of cherry, fig, and cedar.

Sour Then Sweet

Preparation time:	Cooking time:	Servings:
10 minutes	30 minutes	3

Ingredients

- 4 cups Brined Cucumber Ribbons
- 2 cups Spiced Candied Nuts
- 8 ounces SeaHive cheddar (or any mild white cheddar)
- 8 ounces pickled herring
- 8 ounces mascarpone
- ¼ cup honey
- 2 Granny Smith apples, cored and sliced
- 1 sourdough baguette
- You will also need: a large board, a small cheese knife, a pint-size canning jar, 2 small cocktail forks, a small dish, a small bowl, a small spreading knife or spoon, a small honey jar, a honey wand

Directions

Prepare the brined cucumber ribbons and spiced candied nuts according to the recipes. The cucumbers can be prepared up to a week ahead of time and the nuts up to 3 months.

Place the cheddar in the bottom right corner of the board with a small cheese knife next to it.

Place the brined cucumber ribbons in a pint-size jar below the top left corner. Add a small cocktail fork to the jar.

Put the pickled herring into a small dish with a cocktail fork, and place it next to the cucumber ribbons but slightly offset.

In the top center of the board, place the mascarpone in a bowl with a small spreading knife or spoon.

Put the honey in a small jar with a honey wand, and place it to the right of the mascarpone.

Sprinkle the candied nuts near the cheddar in the bottom center of the board.

Place the Granny Smith slices in the center of the board.

Tear the baguette into large pieces and place them along the top right side of the board near the herring.

Drink pairing: A green appletini is the perfect sour and sweet drink to accompany this arrangement. In a cocktail shaker, combine 1 ounce Smirnoff Green Apple Vodka, ½ ounce sour mix, 3 ounces apple cider, and some ice cubes. Shake well, then strain into a cocktail glass and coat the rim with a 1-to-2 salt-to-sugar ratio. Garnish with a small wedge of Granny Smith apple.

Chapter 4: Evening Boards

Beef Noodle Egg Rolls

Preparation time:	Cooking time:	Servings:
10 minutes	30 minutes	4

Ingredients

- 1 pound ground beef
- ½ cup dry Chow Mein noodles
- 2 celery stalks, finely chopped
- 3 cloves garlic, minced
- 2 tablespoons fresh ginger, grated
- 1 cup cabbage, shredded
- 2 green onions, chopped
- 3 tablespoons soy sauce
- 1 tablespoon Hoisin sauce
- 1 teaspoon black pepper
- Extra light olive oil
- 12 egg roll wrappers

Directions

Soak Chow Mein in warm water.

Heat oil in a skillet over medium heat.

Add garlic and onion, and stir-fry for 30 seconds to a minute until tender and fragrant. Add ground beef, brown, and remove from heat.

Add cabbage, Chow Mein noodles, and ginger to the skillet along with hoisin sauce, pepper, and soy sauce.

Place one heaping tablespoon of filling about three inches above the bottom corner, roll the bottom corner over the wrapper and fold over the left side and then the right side over the wrapper, continue to roll up to one inch below the top corner, brush the top edges with water and flour mixture and seal wrapper, repeat.

Fill a heavy frying pot halfway with oil, or you can also fry the egg rolls in a wok. Let the oil reach 350°F. Deep fry egg rolls until golden brown, about 1-2 minutes per side. You can also use a deep-frying machine.

Serve with your favorite dipping sauce.

Mushrooms and Beef Egg Roll

Preparation time:	Cooking time:	Servings:
10 minutes	30 minutes	10

Ingredients

- 1 onion, diced
- 1 tablespoon olive oil
- 2 baby Bella mushrooms, chopped
- ½ pound ground beef
- 4 teaspoons soya sauce
- 1 cup green cabbage, shredded
- 1 teaspoon chili garlic sauce
- 2 teaspoons ground black pepper, fresh
- 10 egg roll wrappers defrosted
- 1 teaspoon sesame oil
- 1 tablespoon water, 1 egg, beaten together
- Oil for frying

Directions

In a frying pan or a wok, warm the olive oil on medium heat. Add the beef.

Cook the beef till it browns, around 8-10 minutes.

Add onions, mushrooms, and cabbage to the pan. Stir-fry for another 5 minutes.

Remove the pan from the heat, and add soya sauce, chili garlic sauce, and sesame oil.

Take an egg roll wrap and place it on a dry and flat surface.

Place around 2-3 tablespoons of the mixture in the middle of the wrap.

Roll the wrap tightly and seal the ends using the egg and water mixture.

Do the same for all the wraps.

Once the oil has heated to 350°F177°C, fry the egg rolls in batches. Do not overcrowd the saucepan.

Fry on all sides till golden and crisp.

Beef and Caramelized Scallion Fried Dumplings

Preparation time:	Cooking time:	Servings:
10 minutes	30 minutes	4

Ingredients

- ¾ pound ground beef
- 1 cup beans sprouts, roughly chopped
- 3 green onions, finely chopped
- 1 tablespoon ginger, grated
- 4 tablespoons low-sodium soy sauce
- 1 teaspoon black pepper
- 1 egg, beaten
- Extra light olive oil
- 14 dumpling wrappers

Directions

Heat the oil over medium heat, add scallions, sauté for 30 seconds.

Sprinkle scallions with brown sugar, and give a quick sauté.

Add ground beef and brown.

Add ginger, scallions, sauté for a minute.

Add soy sauce, black pepper, mung bean sprouts, and green cabbage, mix and remove from heat.

Bring the bottom half up over the filling to meet the top half and pinch the two halves together in the center, then pinch together the sides.

Place dumplings on a plate and cover them with a slightly damp cloth to ensure they do not dry out.

Fill a large pot of water up halfway over medium heat and bring to a boil.

Drop a batch of dumplings into the water and cook for 10 minutes. Leave raw dumplings under a damp cloth.

Serve warm with a dipping sauce like the spicy peanut sauce.

Cheese and Beef Chips

Preparation time:	Cooking time:	Servings:
10 minutes	30 minutes	4

Ingredients

- ½ pound lean ground beef
- Salt and pepper to taste
- 1½ cups shredded cheddar cheese
- 1 teaspoon dried oregano
- 1 teaspoon dried basil
- ½ teaspoon garlic powder
- 1 teaspoon chili flakes
- 1 teaspoon paprika
- 3 tablespoons olive oil

Directions

Add the ground meat, salt, and pepper, cheese, oregano, basil, garlic powder, chili flakes, and paprika to a large bowl.

Mix until everything is combined.

Grease a 15-inch casserole pan or skillet with olive oil and spread the mixture evenly into it with an offset spatula.

Let cool slightly and cut as desired

Cheeseburger Dip

Preparation time:	Cooking time:	Servings:
10 minutes	30 minutes	4

Nutrition: Calories 137, Fat 5.7, Fiber 10.9, Carbs 21.2, Protein 4.2

Ingredients

- 2 tablespoons olive oil
- ½ pound lean ground beef
- Salt and pepper to taste
- 1 cup sour cream
- 2 cups shredded provolone cheese
- 1 teaspoon freshly chopped thyme
- 1 teaspoon dried oregano
- ½ cup cream cheese
- ½ cup heavy cream

Directions

Warm the olive oil in a pan.

Add the ground beef and cook for 10 minutes.

Stir in the sour cream, cheese, thyme, oregano, and cream cheese.

Pour in the heavy cream and transfer the mixture to a 9×13 baking dish.

Cook in a preheated oven at 350°F (180°C) for about 15–20 minutes.

Serve with your favorite tortilla chips.

Ground Beef Canapés

Nutrition: Calories 357, Fat 23.7, Fiber 3.3, Carbs 11.4, Protein 26.3

Preparation time:	Cooking time:	Servings:
10 minutes	60 minutes	4

Ingredients

- 3 tablespoons olive oil
- 1 pound of lean ground beef
- Salt and pepper to taste
- 1 teaspoon dried thyme
- 1 teaspoon dried basil
- 1 tablespoon BBQ sauce
- 1 teaspoon Dijon mustard
- 1 cup tomato sauce
- 3 tablespoons freshly chopped parsley
- 7 ounces crackers

Directions

Using a nonstick pan heat the butter

Add the ground beef and cook it for about 10 minutes.

Season with salt and pepper, thyme, basil, BBQ sauce, Dijon mustard, and tomato sauce.

Cook for 5 minutes and sprinkle in the parsley.

Let cool completely and serve on.

Beef Patty Lettuce Wraps

Preparation time:	Cooking time:	Servings:
10 minutes	60 minutes	4

Ingredients

- 8 Bibb lettuce leaves
- ½ avocado
- 1 pound 90% lean ground beef
- ¼ teaspoon pepper
- ½ teaspoon salt
- ⅓ cup feta cheese, crumbled
- 2 tablespoons low-carb mayonnaise
- ¼ cup chopped red onion
- Chopped cherry tomatoes (optional)
- ½ avocados

Directions

Add the beef in, salt, and pepper to a mixing bowl; mix well.

Prepare 8 patties from the mixture.

Preheat the grill to medium-high heat.

Grill the patties for 4 minutes on each side until evenly brown.

Arrange the lettuce leaves and place the patties over them.

In a bowl, combine the mayonnaise and feta cheese. Spread over the patties.

Top with red onion, avocado, and optionally with tomatoes. Serve fresh.

Nutrition: Calories 357, Fat 23.7, Fiber 3.3, Carbs 11.4, Protein 26.3

Runza

Preparation time:	Cooking time:	Servings:
10 minutes	60 minutes	4

Ingredients

- 2 tablespoons olive oil
- 1 medium onion, finely diced
- 1 garlic clove, minced
- 1 pound of lean ground beef
- 1 cup of prepared sauerkraut, with the juices
- ½ small green cabbage, shredded
- Salt and pepper
- Frozen or fresh bread dough for 2 loaves, thawed if frozen
- 1 egg
- 4 tablespoons water
- Melted butter (optional)

Directions

Place a cast-iron Dutch oven or deep pan over medium heat and add the olive oil. Sauté the garlic and onion until fragrant and translucent, about 1–2 minutes.

Add the ground beef. Using a wooden spoon, break up any lumps and brown for 4–5 minutes until it changes color. Season generously with salt and pepper. Drain the beef mixture to remove excess liquids.

Add the cabbage and sauerkraut.

Stir a few times to combine the ingredients well. Cook on low heat for 2–2½ hours or until the filling has reduced and the cabbage becomes tender. (You can also use a slow cooker and cook on low for 3–4 hours.)

Preheat the oven to 400°F and line a baking sheet with parchment paper

Take the bread dough and roll it out to about ¼ inch thick. Cut into 4×8 inch rectangles.

In a small bowl, mix the egg with the water to make an egg wash.

Spoon about ½ cup of the ground beef mixture into the center of each runza. Fold the dough pieces over and pinch to seal.

Place on the baking sheet, seam side down. Brush the bread pockets lightly with the egg wash.

Bake the bread pockets for 20 minutes or until you see that the pastry has risen. Reduce heat to 350°F and bake for another 15–20 minutes until golden brown.

If desired, brush each runza lightly with some melted butter as soon as they are out of the oven. Allow to cool slightly before serving.

Nutrition: Calories 360, Fat 22.9, Fiber 0.8, Carbs 2.9, Protein 33.6

Sage Venison Sausage

Preparation time:	Cooking time:	Servings:
10 minutes	30 minutes	4

Ingredients

- 2 pounds ground venison
- 2 teaspoons salt
- 1 teaspoon dried parsley
- 1 teaspoon ground sage
- ½ teaspoon pepper
- ½ teaspoon dried thyme
- ½ teaspoon coriander
- ¼ teaspoon nutmeg
- ½ teaspoon Accent
- ¼ teaspoon ground red pepper
- ¼ cup hot water

Directions

Combine all the spices and water. Add ground venison and mix well. It may be cooked immediately or frozen.

Sweet Italian Venison Sausage

Preparation time:	Cooking time:	Servings:
10 minutes	30 minutes	4

Ingredients

- 4 pounds ground venison
- 1 pound ground pork
- 2 tablespoons salt
- 1 cup water
- ½ tablespoon cracked fennel seed
- 1 teaspoon pepper
- ½ tablespoon brown sugar
- ½ teaspoon caraway seed
- ½ tablespoon coriander
- 1 ½ teaspoon crushed red pepper

Directions

Mix spices into water. Add venison and pork. Mix well. It may be cooked immediately or frozen.

Summer Sausage

Preparation time:	Cooking time:	Servings:
10 minutes	30 minutes	4

Ingredients

- 2 pounds ground venison
- 2 tablespoons tender quick salt
- 1 teaspoon liquid smoke
- ¼ teaspoon pepper
- ¼ teaspoon garlic powder
- ¼ teaspoon onion powder
- ¾ teaspoon mustard powder
- 1 cup water

Directions

Mix all ingredients. Place mixture in a container with a lid and refrigerate for 24 hours. Shape into 2 rolls. Place on a cake rack and place rack on a cookie sheet. Bake for 1 ½ hour at 350 degrees.

Nutrition: Calories 357, Fat 23.7, Fiber 3.3, Carbs 11.4, Protein 26.3

Soy Sauce Stewed Eggs

Preparation time:	Cooking time:	Servings:
10 minutes	40 minutes	3

Ingredients

- 3-4 hard boiled eggs, peeled
- 2 cups of water
- 1/2 cup soy sauce
- 1 tablespoon brown sugar
- 1/4 tablespoon five-spice powder

Directions

Add water, soy sauce, sugar, and spice powder to a saucepan and bring the mixture to a simmer.

Add peeled eggs. Use a spoon to base the eggs to coat them evenly on all sides.

Simmer the eggs in the mixture for 15-20 minutes.

Transfer eggs to a bowl and add a little bit of the sauce over it. Let them rest for 5-10 minutes.

Serve soy sauce stewed eggs warm or cold with ramen.

Teriyaki Pork Tenderloin

Preparation time:	Cooking time:	Servings:
10 minutes	40 minutes	3

Ingredients

- 1/4 cup soy sauce

- 1/4 cup mirin

- 1 tablespoon brown sugar

- 1/2 cup water

- 1 tablespoon vegetable oil

- 1 1/2 lbs. pork tenderloin, rinse and pat dry with paper towels

Directions

Mix brown sugar, mirin, soy sauce, and water in a bowl.

Heat oil in a deep fry pan. Brown each side of pork tenderloin for 5 minutes.

Pour the sauce into the pan. Cover with lid, switch heat to medium-low, and cook for 30 minutes, turning once halfway through. If needed, add another 1/4 cup water to avoid burning.

Remove pork from the pan and slice after it has cooled enough.

Cha Shu Pork

Preparation time:	Cooking time:	Servings:
10 minutes	40 minutes	3

Ingredients

- 2 lbs. slab pork shoulder
- 10 cups water
- 4 1/4 cups dark soy sauce
- 2 1/2 cups sugar
- 3/4 cup mirin
- 1 clove garlic
- 1 green onion, chopped
- 1 tablespoon ginger, grated

Directions

Cut pork into 4-5-inch-wide long strips, rolled up into a round bundle, and trussed with cooking string to keep its shape.

Mix shoyu, water, mirin, sugar, garlic, onion, ginger, and pork in a large pot. Bring to a boil, switch heat to low, and simmer for 4 hours until pork is tender. Skim any scum off the surface.

Check the doneness of pork with a thick wooden skewer. Insert it into the center of the meat. The pork is done when it comes out clean. Leave it to cool to room temperature. Remove string when it's chilled.

Put the pork in the liquid in the fridge to rest for 2 hours or overnight (it will make the meat easier to slice). Do not throw the liquid away – save it for other ramen recipes!

Slice pork into ¼-inch rounds and sauté in a skillet for 1-2 minutes to render the fat and make slices crispy before serving on top of ramen.

Tamagoyaki Japanese Omelet

Preparation time:	Cooking time:	Servings:
10 minutes	40 minutes	3

Ingredients

- 4 eggs
- 1 tablespoon soy sauce
- 1 tablespoon mirin
- 1 tablespoon sugar
- 1 pinch of salt
- cooking oil, as needed

Directions

Beat eggs well in a bowl using a fork, or chopsticks.

Add soy sauce, mirin, sugar, and salt to the egg mixture.

Add cooking oil to a pan and bring it up to medium heat. Keep some paper towels handy to help keep the pan oiled during cooking.

Pour a little egg mixture into the heated pan. Once it has cooked slightly and the top is still slightly uncooked, push it over to the other side of the pan.

Oil the pan with a paper towel and add another small amount of the egg mixture to the pan. Wait until it's cooked a little and roll the first bit of egg over the mixture that has been just put in the pan until you get a small roll of the egg. Keep adding the egg in new layers until you have used it all up.

Remove and let it cool before slicing.

Tokushima Ramen

Preparation time:	Cooking time:	Servings:
10 minutes	40 minutes	3

Ingredients

- 4 portions uncooked noodles

- 300 grams thinly sliced pork belly

- 1 bag bean sprouts

- 1/2 bunch chopped green onion

- 2 tablespoons of Weipa

- 2 tablespoons soy sauce

- 1 tablespoon sugar

- 2 tablespoons sake

- 2 tablespoons soy sauce

- 4 halved ramen eggs

Directions

Boil 4 cups of water. Add Weipa and 2 tablespoons of soy sauce. Cook according to the directions on the Weipa can.

Meanwhile, heat sesame oil in a frying pan and stir-fry bean sprouts for 2 minutes. Season them with salt and pepper. Set aside bean sprouts and wipe out the pan.

Add vegetable oil and stir-fry the sliced pork. When the meat changes color from all sides, add 2 tablespoons of soy sauce, sugar, and sake.

Cook noodles in another pot following the directions on the package.

Ladle the soup base in bowls and add noodles, sprouts, pork belly, and sprinkle with chopped green onions. Top with a halved ramen egg and serve.

Country Casserole

Preparation time:	Cooking time:	Servings:
10 minutes	40 minutes	3

Ingredients

- 3/4 cup elbow macaroni

- 1 pound ground turkey

- 1 (15 ounces) can of baked beans with pork

- 1/2 cup chopped green pepper

- 1 (10 ounces) can refrigerated biscuit dough

- 1 (5.5 ounces) can tomato-vegetable juice cocktail

- salt and pepper to taste

- 6 slices American cheese

Direction

Turn the oven to 375°F (190°C) to preheat. Bring lightly salted water in a small saucepan to a boil. Cook macaroni in boiling water until al dente for 8 minutes. Drain pasta; put to one side.

In a large skillet, put green pepper and ground beef. Sauté over medium-high heat until browned. Drain drippings and return the skillet to heat. Mix in pepper, salt, vegetable juice, cooked macaroni, and beans. Cook through; pour the mixture into a 9-inch square casserole dish or baking dish. Split biscuits apart and slice into quarters. Arrange biscuits on a baking sheet.

Bake the casserole without covering and the biscuits for 15 minutes at the same time in the preheated oven until biscuits are cooked through. Take the casserole out of the oven just before the biscuits are done; place slices of cheese over top of the casserole dish. Place back into the oven to melt.

Take the mixture in the casserole dish out onto serving plates and pat a couple of biscuit quarters into each serving to serve.

Wakayama Ramen

Preparation time:	Cooking time:	Servings:
10 minutes	40 minutes	3

Ingredients

For the broth:

- 4 cups pork broth
- 2 1/2 tablespoons soy sauce
- 1 tablespoon of sake
- 1 tablespoon bonito flakes
- 2 teaspoons roasted sesame oil

For the toppings:

- 6 Naruto fish cake slices
- 1/4 lb. Cha Shu, sliced
- 3 green onions, sliced
- 1 soft boiled ramen egg
- 2 portions ramen noodles
- For the pickled mackerel:
- 1/2 lb. mackerel (or herring)
- 2 1/2 cups water
- 1/2 cup salt
- 1 cup white vinegar
- 1/6 cup sugar
- 1 tablespoon miso paste
- 1 teaspoon black peppercorns

Directions

To prepare mackerel, heat 2 cups of water enough to dissolve the salt. Then, let it cool to room temperature. Submerge mackerel in the brine in the jar.

Boil the remaining 1/2 cup water, vinegar, pepper, and sugar in another pot. Add miso once it cools.

When the pickling liquid is cool enough (room temperature), pour it over brine and fish and in a jar. Close and leave overnight.

Mix broth ingredients in a pot and simmer for 30 minutes on medium-low heat. Strain bonito flakes out before serving.

Boil Naruto fish cake for 5 minutes. Take out of the water and slice thinly.

Cook noodles following directions in the recipe or on the package. Strain.

Add broth to the bowl, then noodles, and toppings. Serve fish on the side.

Sapporo Miso Ramen

Preparation time:	Cooking time:	Servings:
10 minutes	40 minutes	3

Ingredients

For the ramen:

- 6 oz. soybean sprouts (ends trimmed)
- 12 oz. ramen
- 1 teaspoon sesame oil
- 2 tablespoons vegetable oil
- 3 green onions, sliced
- 1/3 cup Shiro miso
- 1/3 cup aka miso

For the toppings:

- 12 slices of teriyaki pork tenderloin
- 1 cup corn kernels
- 4 ramen eggs, sliced into half lengthwise
- 4 tablespoon chili bamboo shoots
- 2 green onions, finely sliced
- Garlic chili oil, to taste
- 2 sheets nori

For the broth:

- 1 lb. pork bones
- 10 cups water
- 1-inch ginger, peeled and smashed
- For the corn kernels:
- 2 tablespoons butter
- 1 cup frozen corn kernels
- For the garlic chili oil:
- 2 cloves garlic, minced
- 1 teaspoon red pepper flakes
- 3 tablespoons vegetable oil

Directions

Bring one half a pot of water to boil. Add pork bones and boil them for 5 minutes. Take out the bones with thongs and rinse off scum. Discard water and rinse the pot.

Pour 10 cups of water into the pot and bring to a boil. Add ginger and bones to the pot. Once it is boiling, switch heat to low and simmer for 2 hours.

Melt butter in a saucepan. Add corn kernels and cook them for 3 minutes. Remove and set aside.

Mix pepper flakes, garlic, and oil in a small microwavable dish. Microwave for 1 minute 30 seconds. Remove and set aside.

Bring one more large pot of water to boil. Scald bean sprouts for 20 seconds. Remove and set aside.

Add noodles and cook according to instructions. Drain noodles and rinse under cold water. Add sesame oil and toss.

Divide noodles into 4 bowls. Top with teriyaki pork tenderloin, bean sprouts, corn kernels, and chili bamboo shoots.

Add Shiro and miso in a bowl. Pour 1 cup boiling stock over miso. Mix to melt miso and set aside.

Add 2 tablespoons of oil into a large pot and heat it. Add green onions and cook for 2 minutes.

Add in 8 cups of stock in a pot. When it's boiling, reduce heat to low.

Gradually stir in melted miso back into the pot. Do not let it boil. Turn off heat.

Pour miso over noodles in each bowl. Sprinkle with green onions and garlic chili oil before serving

Hiyashi Chuka Cold Ramen

Preparation time:	Cooking time:	Servings:
10 minutes	40 minutes	3

Ingredients

For the ramen:

- 2 portions ramen noodles
- 1/2 cucumber, thinly sliced
- 4 sticks crab meat, shredded into thin strips
- 1/4 lb. shrimp, shelled and deveined
- 1/2 tomato, sliced
- 50 g ham, cut into strips
- 2 eggs

For the sesame dressing:

- 1 teaspoon Chicken Gara soup stock powder
- 100 ml hot water
- 4 tablespoon white sesame seeds paste
- 2 tablespoons soy sauce
- 3 tablespoons sugar
- 3 tablespoons rice wine vinegar
- 2 teaspoons sesame oil
- 2 teaspoons sesame seeds

For the soy sauce vinaigrette:

- 1 teaspoon Chicken Gara soup stock powder
- 1/3 cup ml hot water
- 6 tablespoon soy sauce
- 3 tablespoons vinegar
- 3 tablespoons sugar
- 2 tablespoons sesame seed oil

For the garnish:

- 2 tablespoons pickled ginger
- 1 tablespoon chopped scallions
- 1 tablespoon Japanese kewpie mayonnaise
- 1/2 teaspoon mustard
- 1 teaspoon white sesame seeds

Directions

Mix chicken Gara powder and hot water until fully dissolved in a bowl.

Add remaining ingredients for soy sauce vinaigrette and mix. Chill in the fridge.

Fry eggs in a thin layer and cut them into thin strips. Set it aside to cool down.

Cook noodles per instructions and let cool.

Assemble by placing chilled noodles in a bowl, then top with shrimp, crab meat, egg, cucumber, tomato, and ham.

Garnish with ginger, lemon slice, and scallion. Pour sesame dressing over the top and sprinkle with sesame seeds.

Serve with Japanese mayonnaise and mustard.

Okinawa Soba

Preparation time:	Cooking time:	Servings:
10 minutes	40 minutes	3

Ingredients

For the broth:

- 14 oz. pork belly block
- 4 cups water for pre-boiling
- 6 cups water for the broth

For the Katsuo Dashi:

- 2 cups water
- 1 cup katsuobushi
- For the soup broth:
- 1/2 tablespoon sea salt
- 2 teaspoons soy sauce
- For the stewed pork belly:
- 2 tablespoons black sugar
- 2 tablespoons awamori
- 2 tablespoons soy sauce
- 2 tablespoons water

For the Okinawa Soba:

- 2 servings noodles
- green onion/scallion, chopped, to taste
- sliced fish cakes, to taste

Directions

Put pork belly in a large pot and add enough water to cover the meat. Bring the water to a boil.

Once boiling, switch heat to low and simmer for 3-5 minutes, until it foams and scum floats on the surface. Drain and rinse the pork and the pot under running water.

Return meat to the same pot, and add 6 cups of water. Bring it to a boil.

When it's boiling, simmer for 1 hour, skimming off scum and foam from the surface.

At the same time, bring 2 cups of water to a boil in a small saucepan. Turn heat to low, add katsuobushi, and let simmer for 15 seconds. Turn off heat. Set aside to steep until ready to use.

Remove pork from the pot and cover it with foil. Set aside to cool.

Strain the broth through a fine sieve. Put 4 cups of pork broth back in the pot.

Strain bonito flakes water through the sieve. Bring the broth to a boil.

Once boiling, switch to low heat and add 2 teaspoons soy sauce and 1 tablespoon salt. Mix well and adjust salt if needed. Turn off and cover the pot with a lid. Set aside.

When pork belly is cool enough, cut into thin 1-inch slices.

Add 2 tablespoons of black sugar, 2 tablespoons of awamori, 2 tablespoons soy sauce, and 2 tablespoons of water. Mix well and bring to a boil. Lower heat and add pork slices, quickly coating with sauce.

Cover with lid and cook for 25-30 minutes on low, until sauce has almost evaporated.

Cook noodles according to the package directions. Drain the noodles.

Place the noodles in a bowl. Pour soup broth over the noodles and top with pork belly slices, green onions, and fish cake.

Homemade Tonkotsu Ramen

Preparation time:	Cooking time:	Servings:
10 minutes	40 minutes	3

Ingredients

For the broth:

- 6 lbs. pork bones
- 1 onion, peeled and halved

For the miso tare:

- 1/2 cup Shiro miso
- 1/4 cup sake
- 1/4 cup mirin
- 1 teaspoon kosher salt

For the ramen:

- 8 cups homemade pork broth
- 12 oz. dried ramen noodles
- 4 large hard-boiled eggs
- 12 Cha Shu pork slices
- 2 oz. dried shiitake mushrooms
- 1/2 cup bamboo shoots
- 1 green onion, sliced
- 4 nori sheets

Directions

Cover pork bones with cold water in a large stockpot. Bring to a boil over medium heat, then discard water and rinse bones in cold water. Return bones to the stockpot, cover with water and bring to a boil. Then lower heat to medium.

Add onion, and cover the pot. Cook for 10-12 hours over medium heat, adding water as needed to keep the bones covered.

Remove bones, strain the broth, and let it cool to room temperature.

Add miso, sake, mirin, and salt into a small saucepan. Bring to a simmer and cook for 5 minutes. Set aside.

Cook noodles, following directions on the package.

Rehydrate mushrooms in boiling water and set them aside.

Heat a large skillet and brown sliced pork on all sides.

Divide the miso tare into four bowls. Top with 1/2 cup broth and mix well.

Add noodles and 1 1/2 cups broth.

Top with egg, nori, mushrooms, pork, and green onions.

Can be stored for 4 months in the freezer.

Tonkotsu Miso Ramen

Preparation time:	Cooking time:	Servings:
10 minutes	40 minutes	3

Ingredients

For the broth:

- 2 1/2 cups Tonkotsu base
- 2 tablespoons white miso
- 1 tablespoon tahini
- 2 teaspoons sesame oil
- 2 cloves garlic, grated
- 1/2 cup water
- 2 tablespoons pork fat, minced

For the toppings:

- 1 tablespoon ground sesame seeds
- 1/2 ramen noodles
- 12 Cha Shu pork slices
- garlic chives
- 1 bunch scallions, chopped
- 1/4 cup sweet corn
- 2 oz. dried shiitake mushrooms, rehydrated and sliced
- 1 ramen egg
- 2 large dried scallops

Directions

Heat Tonkotsu Base in a medium saucepan.

Mix miso, sesame oil, tahini, and garlic in a small bowl, whisk in water. Pour the mixture into a hot Tonkotsu Base and whisk well. Once it's creamy and smooth without any chunks, add pork fat and whisk. Adjust salt to taste. If it's too concentrated, thin it out with water.

Divide cooked noodles between two bowls. Add ground sesame seeds to the soup and whisk one more time, then pour over noodles.

Top with listed or toppings and grate dried scallop over each bowl before serving.

Creamy Tonkotsu Ramen

Preparation time:	Cooking time:	Servings:
10 minutes	40 minutes	3

Ingredients

- 1 large onion, skin on, chopped
- 1 3-inch knob ginger, chopped
- 2 whole leeks, washed and chopped
- 2 dozen scallions, chopped
- 6 halved ramen eggs
- 2 tablespoons vegetable oil
- 12 garlic cloves
- 6 oz. enoki mushrooms
- 1 lb. slab pork fatback
- 2 lbs. chicken carcasses and backs, skin and fat removed
- 3 lbs. pig trotters, cut crosswise into 1-inch disks

Directions

Heat oil in a nonstick skillet over high heat. Add garlic, onions, and ginger. Cook for 15 minutes, tossing occasionally. Set aside.

Add chicken and pork bones to a large stockpot and cover with cold water. Bring to a boil over high heat, then remove from heat and discard water.

Wash all bones under cold water, removing coagulated blood or any bits of dark marrow. Bones should become uniform grey or white after scrubbing.

Return bones to pot with pork fatback, scallion whites, charred vegetables, leeks, and mushrooms. Cover with cold water. Bring to a rolling boil over high heat, skimming off any scum. Wipe any scum off from around the rim of the pot with a paper towel. Switch heat to low, let simmer and place a heavy lid on top.

Check the broth after 15 minutes. If it's not a slow rolling boil, increase or decrease the heat to adjust the boiling speed. Boil for 4 hours, until fatback is fully tender.

Remove pork fat with a slotted spatula and place it in a sealed container in the fridge.

Cover the pot and cook for 6-8 hours, until broth is opaque with the texture of light cream, adding more water to keep bones covered.

When broth is ready, turn to high heat and cook until reduced to 3 quarts. Strain into a clean pot. Repeat if you want cleaner broth. Discard any solids and fat with a ladle. Roughly chop pork fatback and whisk into broth.

To serve, season soup with condiments of choice and serve with cooked ramen noodles and preferable toppings.

Tonkotsu Toridashi Ramen

Preparation time:	Cooking time:	Servings:
10 minutes	40 minutes	3

Ingredients

- 10 oz. ramen noodles

- 2 tablespoon sesame oil

- 10 shiitake mushrooms, cut into slithers

- 4 1/2 pints toridashi stock

- 1oz. ginger, cut into 4 slices

- 3 ½ oz. shimeji mushrooms

- 1 carrot, cut into matchsticks

- 7 oz. soya bean sprouts

- 1 1/2 bamboo shoots, sliced

- 2 garlic cloves, sliced

- 3 ½ oz. enoki mushrooms

- 16 slices Cha Shu pork

- 4 spring onion, cut on the diagonal

- 7 oz. Choi Sum, trimmed and cut in half

- 1 red chili, finely sliced on a diagonal

- 4 whole tomago eggs, halved

For the serving:

- Japanese chili oil

- shichimi togarashi (Japanese seven-spice seasoning)

- dried tuna flakes

For the Toridashi stock:

- 3lb 5oz. chicken wings

- 3lb 5oz. pork bones

- 10g piece dried kombu

- 2 thick slices of fresh root ginger

- 9 oz. of sake

- 1 medium onion, cut in half

- 1oz. bonito flakes (katsuobushi)

- 6 dried shiitake mushrooms

Directions

Preheat the oven to 375°F.

Arrange pork bones and chicken wings in a roasting pan and roast for 30-40 minutes, turning them halfway through, until golden brown.

Place wings and bones in a large sieve, then pour boiling water over bones to remove excess grease.

While chicken is in the oven, rinse kombu under cold water. Soak kombu in a large pot for 30 minutes in 4 1/2 pints cold water.

Remove kombu from water and cut into three long strips. Return to the stockpot and bring to a simmer. Remove from heat and discard kombu.

Add wings, bones, and all remaining ingredients to kombu water. Bring it to a boil, cover with a lid and simmer for 2 hours on low.

Strain the stock through a fine-mesh strainer. Leave for 10 minutes to drain, cool, and set in the fridge until you need it.

Cook noodles following the directions on the packet. Drain and drizzle with sesame oil.

Heat stock in a pan with ginger, garlic, mushrooms, and carrots. Simmer for 5-8 minutes. Add shimeji mushrooms.

Place noodles, bamboo shoots, beansprouts, enoki mushrooms, Choi Sum, and sliced pork in serving bowls. Ladle stock over the noodles. Sprinkle with spring onions, shichimi togarashi, and sliced chili. Top with halved tamago egg and serve.

Tonkotsu Shio Ramen

Preparation time:	Cooking time:	Servings:
10 minutes	40 minutes	3

Ingredients

- 10 oz. ramen noodles

- 4 lbs. pork feet, cut to expose the bone marrow

- 6 ramen eggs

- 12 Cha Shu pork slices

- 1 cup sweet corn

- 1 bunch chopped green onion

For the Shio tare:

- 2 tablespoons sea salt

- 2 tablespoons sake

- 1 tablespoon mirin

- 2 teaspoons sesame oil

- 1 teaspoon soy sauce

- 1 garlic clove, crushed

Directions

Place pork feet in a big pot and cover with water (1-2 inches above the bones). Boil for 15 min, stirring. Remove all the junk from the surface.

Remove from heat and strain the bones. Clean coagulated blood or dark marrow with the end of a chopstick or toothbrush.

Return bones to the pot and cover with water a few inches above them. Bring to a rolling boil, lower the heat and simmer for 16 hours.

Mix all tare ingredients and add a spoonful to the bottom of each serving bowl. Add the broth and season with more tare if needed.

Boil noodles according to the directions on a package and drain them.

Divide noodles between bowls, top with sliced pork, ramen egg, sweet corn, and chopped green onion.

Yummy Pork Noodle Casserole

Preparation time:	Cooking time:	Servings:
10 minutes	40 minutes	3

Ingredients

- 2 cups egg noodles

- cooking spray

- 3 tablespoons butter

- 1/4 cup chopped onion

- 1/4 cup chopped celery

- 1/4 cup chopped carrots

- 1/4 cup chopped red bell pepper

- 2 (10.75 ounces) cans condensed cream of chicken soup

- 1/2 cup sour cream, or more to taste

- 2 cups shredded Cheddar cheese

- 1 (8 ounces) can whole kernel corn, drained

- 3 cups cubed cooked pork

- 1 teaspoon salt

- 1/4 teaspoon ground black pepper

- 1/2 cup dry bread crumbs (optional)

Direction

Bring lightly salted water in a big pot over high heat to a rolling boil. When water is boiling, mix in egg noodles, and bring back to a boil. Cook pasta without a cover for 5 minutes, mixing from time to time, till noodles have cooked through, yet are firm to the bite. Drain thoroughly in a colander placed in the sink.

Preheat the oven to 175 °C or 350 °F. With cooking spray, coat a 9x13-inch baking pan.

In a skillet, liquify the butter over moderate heat. Mix in red bell pepper, carrots, celery, and onion; cook and mix for 5 minutes till onion becomes translucent and has softened. Mix in cooked pork, corn, Cheddar cheese, sour cream, cream of chicken soup, and noodles, then add black pepper and salt to season. Turn mixture onto the prepped baking dish. Scatter the bread crumbs over top.

In the prepped oven, bake for 30 to 35 minutes till bubbly.

Fast Miso Ramen

Preparation time:	Cooking time:	Servings:
10 minutes	40 minutes	3

Ingredients

- 6 oz. of noodles
- 2 tablespoons of miso paste
- 2 cloves of garlic
- 1 tablespoon of sambal oelek
- 2½ cups of vegetable broth
- 2 oz. of mung bean sprouts
- 4 small discs of roast pork (cooked)
- 4 surimi pieces
- 1 oz. of corn
- 2 seaweed leaves
- 2 spring onions
- Vegetable oil

Instructions

Cook the ramen noodles.

Heat the oil in the saucepan. Add garlic and sambal oelek. Before it turns brown, add the broth and stir in the miso paste.

Rinse the mung bean seedlings with water and put them briefly in the broth, as well as the roast pork and the surimi pieces, so that they become warm.

Cut the spring onions into small pieces.

Place the noodles in a large bowl. Arrange everything in a circle except the spring onions. Pour in the broth from the center (let it get hot again beforehand). Finally, put the spring onions in the middle.

Instant Pot Tonkotsu Ramen

Preparation time:	Cooking time:	Servings:
10 minutes	40 minutes	3

Ingredients

For the broth:

- 3 lbs. pork bones, with some meat
- 1 onion, peeled and halved
- 4 cloves garlic
- 1-inch ginger root, peeled

For the ramen:

- 8 cups Tonkotsu pork broth
- 12 oz. dried or fresh ramen noodles
- 12 slices Cha Shu pork slices
- 4 large ramen eggs
- 3 oz. dried shiitake ore enoki mushrooms, rehydrated
- 1/2 cup bamboo shoots, if desired
- 1/2 cup sweet corn, if desired
- 1/2 cup green onions, thinly sliced

For the miso tare:

- 1/2 cup Shiro miso
- 1/4 cup of sake
- 1/4 cup mirin
- 1 1/2 teaspoons kosher salt

Directions

Add pork bones to a large stockpot and cover with cold water. Let sit for 12 hours.

Pour 2 cups of water into a large saucepan and bring to a boil over medium-high heat.

Meanwhile, transfer pork bones to a pot, cover them with boiling water, and set to sauté on High. Simmer for 10 minutes and press cancel.

Drain water, place bones in a bowl of cold water, and then remove any fat. Clean the inner pot.

Add garlic, ginger, and onion, then return bones to the inner pot. Fill with water to the 3-4 fill line.

Lock the lid, set the valve to sealed. Cook on High pressure for 90 minutes (manual), then do a natural release.

Mix all ingredients for miso tare in a saucepan and simmer for 5 minutes on low heat.

Boil the ramen noodles per package instructions.

Rehydrate mushrooms in hot water until just softened. Drain mushrooms.

Heat oil in a nonstick skillet over medium heat. Brown pork slices on both sides.

Add 1/4 miso tare to each serving bowl. Add a ladle of tonkotsu broth, noodles and add another ladle of broth. Top with ramen egg, bamboo shoots, Cha Shu pork slices, sweet corn, and chopped green onion.

Singapore Noodles

Preparation time:	Cooking time:	Servings:
10 minutes	40 minutes	5

Ingredients

- 1 pound Vermicelli pasta
- 4 cups water
- 2 breasts boneless chicken
- 2 pork chops
- 2 Garlic cloves
- 3 tablespoons oil
- ½ sliced onion
- 2 sliced carrots
- 2 celery stalks
- 12 ounces shrimps
- 1 cup bean sprouts
- 1 tablespoon soya sauce
- 3 tablespoons curry powder
- ¼ cup water

Directions:

Boil water in a large pot and cook in the vermicelli pasta.

Drain and set aside.

Add oil into a pan and fry the chicken, pork, and garlic clove.

Now add in the sliced onion, sliced carrot, and fry till tender.

Add in the celery and the shrimps.

Mix in the bean sprouts, soya sauce, and curry powder.

Add in the water and let simmer for a few minutes.

Mix in the cooked pasta once the water has reduced.

Mix properly and serve!

Asian Crab and Cucumber Salad

Preparation time:	Cooking time:	Servings:
10 minutes	40 minutes	5

Ingredients

- 1 cucumber, sliced
- salt and ground black pepper to taste
- 1 (8 ounces) package imitation crabmeat, coarsely chopped
- 1 tablespoon white wine vinegar
- 1 tablespoon soy sauce

Direction

In a bowl put cucumber slices; season with pepper and salt. Toss imitation crab meat in. In another bowl, whisk soy sauce and vinegar. Put in the crab and cucumber mixture. Toss till coated.

Chilli Prawn Noodles

Preparation time:	Cooking time:	Servings:
10 minutes	40 minutes	5

Ingredients

- 1 lb. green (raw) prawns, unpeeled
- 2 tablespoons peanut oil
- 2½ cups chicken stock
- 1 clove garlic, crushed
- 2 tablespoons sweet chili sauce (e.g., Lingham's SOS brand)
- 4 tablespoons tomato sauce or ketchup
- ½ teaspoon salt
- 1 teaspoon sugar
- 1 teaspoon corn flour - dissolve in 1 tablespoon water
- 4 spring onions, chopped
- 1 egg white, beaten
- 14 oz. fresh Hokkien noodles

Instructions

Devein prawns by hooking out the black intestinal tract with a fine bamboo skewer. Heat oil in and fry prawns for 1 to 2 minutes until they turn red. Add chicken stock and simmer for 1 minute. Add garlic, chili sauce, tomato sauce, salt, and sugar. Mix well.

Add cornflour paste, bring to boil. Stir for 60 seconds. Add half the spring onion and toss well. Slowly dribble egg white into the sauce (a good trick is to pour it through the tines of a fork), stirring constantly, until the sauce thickens.

Pour boiling water over noodles in a heatproof bowl, leave to stand for 2 minutes, and drain. Arrange on a serving platter and pour prawns and sauce on top. Scatter with remaining spring onion.

Suckling Pig, Jellyfish, and Noodle Salad

Preparation time:	Cooking time:	Servings:
10 minutes	40 minutes	5

Ingredients

- 7 oz. dried jellyfish
- 5 oz. bean thread vermicelli
- 1 tablespoon sesame oil
- 2 spring onions, green part only
- ½ cucumber, peeled
- 1 carrot, peeled
- 2 stalks of celery
- 14 oz. cooked suckling pig (from Chinese barbecued meats shop)
- 1 tablespoon soy sauce
- 1 tablespoon white vinegar
- 1 teaspoon sugar

Instructions

Soak jellyfish in a large pot of water for 24 hours, changing the water 3 or 4 times. Trim each piece of jellyfish then roll them up like a piece of carpet. Trim edges and cut into strips about ½ in wide. Dip strips in boiling water, drain, and let cool. Pat dry with paper towels.

Pour boiling water over noodles in a heatproof bowl, let stand for 3 to 5 minutes and drain. Mix with sesame oil and set aside.

Cut 1 spring onion into 2 in sections, then cut each section into matchsticks and set aside.

Using a teaspoon, scoop and discard seeds from the cucumber. Cut cucumber, carrot, and celery into fine matchsticks. Remove skin from suckling pig and cut into thin shards. Cut the flesh into thin strips and toss lightly through the jellyfish with the cucumber, carrot, celery, and noodles. Add soy sauce, vinegar, sugar, and remaining spring onion, finely chopped, and toss again. Serve on a large, warmed serving platter and scatter the crisp skin over the top.

Singapo re Bee Hoon

Preparation time:	Cooking time:	Servings:
10 minutes	40 minutes	5

Ingredients

- 8 oz. rice vermicelli

- 1 tablespoon vegetable oil

- ½ onion, or 4 shallots, sliced

- 1 egg, lightly beaten

- 1 tablespoon chicken stock or water

- 3 oz. cooked shredded chicken

- 3 oz. char siu (red roast pork), sliced

- 1 tablespoon dark soy sauce

- 1 tablespoon light soy sauce

- 5 oz. prawns (shelled)

- ½ cup bean sprouts

- 2 spring onions, finely chopped

- ½ cup shredded lettuce

- 1 tablespoon crisp-fried shallots (available from Asian grocery stores)

- 1 lemon, quartered

Instructions

Pour boiling water over noodles in a heatproof bowl and let stand for 6 to 7 minutes. Rinse in cold water and drain.

In a wok, fry onions in hot oil until it starts to soften. Add egg and stir until softly cooked. Add drained noodles and stir constantly to coat with egg. Moisten with a little stock and cook for 1 minute, then add chicken, pork, and soy sauces and cook for 2 minutes. Add prawns and cook for 1 minute. Add bean sprouts and spring onion and cook for another minute or two. Serve on a large warmed platter, topped with shredded lettuce, crisp-fried shallots, and lemon wedges for squeezing over the lot.

Chilli Prawn Noodles

Preparation time:	Cooking time:	Servings:
10 minutes	40 minutes	5

Ingredients

- 1 lb. green (raw) prawns, unpeeled
- 2 tablespoons peanut oil
- 2½ cups chicken stock
- 1 clove garlic, crushed
- 2 tablespoons sweet chili sauce (e.g., Lingham's SOS brand)
- 4 tablespoons tomato sauce or ketchup
- ½ teaspoon salt
- 1 teaspoon sugar
- 1 teaspoon corn flour - dissolve in 1 tablespoon water
- 4 spring onions, chopped
- 1 egg white, beaten
- 14 oz. fresh Hokkien noodles

Instructions

Devein prawns by hooking out the black intestinal tract with a fine bamboo skewer. Heat oil in and fry prawns for 1 to 2 minutes until they turn red. Add chicken stock and simmer for 1 minute. Add garlic, chili sauce, tomato sauce, salt, and sugar. Mix well.

Add cornflour paste, bring to boil. Stir for 60 seconds. Add half the spring onion and toss well. Slowly dribble egg white into the sauce (a good trick is to pour it through the tines of a fork), stirring constantly, until the sauce thickens.

Pour boiling water over noodles in a heatproof bowl, leave to stand for 2 minutes, and drain. Arrange on a serving platter and pour prawns and sauce on top. Scatter with remaining spring onion.

Seafood Shio ramen

Ingredients

- 6 oz. of glass noodles
- 2 cups of chicken broth
- 4 shiitake mushrooms
- 4.5 oz. of cod fillet
- 6 king prawns
- 3.5 oz. of tofu
- 1 carrot (preferably thin)
- 4.5 oz. of Chinese cabbage
- 1 spring onion
- 1 tablespoon of sherry (dry)
- 2 tablespoons of soy sauce
- ½ tablespoon of lemon juice
- Cayenne pepper

Instructions

Cut the glass noodles into 4-inch pieces, scald them with boiling water, let them steep for 2 minutes, and drain.

Clean the mushrooms and cut lengthwise into quarters. Rinse fish fillet briefly, pat dry, and cut into bite-size pieces. Remove the shell from the shrimp, leave the tailpieces on and gut them.

Cut the drained tofu into 8 cubes. Peel the carrot and slice it into thin slices. Clean, wash, halve and cut Chinese cabbage into strips of about 1 inch wide. Clean the spring onion and slice it into thin slices.

Bring the broth to a boil. Add all the ingredients except the onions and let cook for 2 minutes. Finally, season with sherry, soy sauce, lemon juice, and cayenne pepper and sprinkle with the spring onions.

Katsu Curry Ramen

Preparation time:	Cooking time:	Servings:
10 minutes	40 minutes	3

Ingredients

- 2 lbs. pork feet
- 2 lbs. pork neck bones
- 2 lbs. pork leg bones
- 2 chicken backbones
- 6 cloves garlic
- 1 cup dried shiitake mushrooms, ground
- 1/4 cup bonito flakes
- 1 3-inch piece ginger
- 1 onion, cut into thirds
- 1 leek, halved lengthwise, sliced crosswise, and rinsed
- 1/4 cup dried anchovy
- 1/4 sheet kombu
- 2 tablespoons salt
- 1 tablespoon sugar
- 2 cubes curry bouillon
- 1 teaspoon fish powder

For the pork katsu:

- 1 egg
- 1 lb. pork loin, sliced into 4 portions
- 1 cup all-purpose flour
- 1 gallon of vegetable oil, for deep-frying
- salt, to taste
- 2 cups panko bread crumbs

For the toppings:

- 4 ramen eggs, halved
- 4 portions fresh ramen noodles
- 1 green onion, chopped
- 2 tablespoons toasted sesame seeds

Directions

Place pork feet and all bones in a large stockpot and cover them with water. Cover with lid and bring to a boil. After 10 minutes, remove from heat and strain the bones. Clean bones under running water. Return cleaned bones into a rinsed stockpot, cover with water and bring to a boil again.

Char leek, ginger, garlic, and onion in a skillet until almost burnt. Set aside.

80

Add charred vegetables, bonito flakes, anchovy, ground mushrooms, and kombu to the pot with the bones. Let it boil for 6 hours on low heat. Boil for 12 hours more, then add some salt, sugar, and fish powder. Simmer for 6 hours on low heat. Strain the stock and back it to the pot.

Then, add 2 quarts of pork broth and curry bouillon to make curry broth. Let it boil and whisk well.

Add oil to a heavy-bottomed pot to 350°F. Tenderize pork loin pieces with the flat end of a meat mallet and salt it. Beat egg and 1 tablespoon water together to create an egg wash. Dredge each portion in flour, then egg wash, then bread crumbs. Fry pork loin for 4-5 minutes or so until golden brown and cooked through. Remove from the pan and let it rest for 1-2 minutes.

Cook noodles following the recipe or package directions, drain, and place in bowls.

Pour hot curry broth over noodles and top with fried pork katsu and halved ramen egg. Sprinkle with sesame seeds, chopped green onions, and serve.

Long–Life Noodles

Preparation time:	Cooking time:	Servings:
10 minutes	20 minutes	3

Ingredients

- 4 spring onions
- 8 dried shiitake mushrooms, soaked
- 1 large e-fu noodle cake, about 11 oz.
- 2 tablespoon soy sauce
- 1 tablespoon oyster sauce
- 1 teaspoon sesame oil
- 1 teaspoon sugar
- ¾ cup chicken stock
- 1 tablespoon peanut oil
- 1 tablespoon grated ginger
- 2 cloves garlic, crushed

Instructions

Finely slice the green tops of the spring onions and reserve. Cut the remainder into matchsticks. Drain mushrooms, discard stems, and slice caps finely.

Cook noodles in boiling water for 3 to 4 minutes. Rinse in cold water and drain well.

Mix soy sauce, oyster sauce, sesame oil, sugar, and chicken stock in a bowl and set aside.

Heat oil and stir fry the ginger and garlic for 1 minute. Add spring onion matchsticks, all the mushrooms, and sauce ingredients and bring to a boil, stirring. Cook for 1 minute. Add noodles and cook for about 2 minutes, or until they have absorbed most of the sauce. Serve immediately, scattered with the spring onion greens.

Shrimp Garlic Ramen

Preparation time:	Cooking time:	Servings:
10 minutes	20 minutes	3

Ingredients

- 4 eggs ramen eggs, halved
- 2 tablespoons avocado oil
- 4 cloves garlic, chopped
- 1 tablespoon ginger, grated
- 2 tablespoons red curry paste
- 4 cups chicken broth
- 1 (13.5 oz.) can coconut milk
- 1 tablespoon fish sauce
- 1 lb. crab clusters
- 2 portions ramen noodles
- 1 lb. shrimp, tails removed, peeled, and deveined
- Kosher salt and pepper, to taste
- 4 lime wedges
- 1 bunch cilantro, chopped
- 1 bunch green onion, chopped

Directions

Cook ginger and garlic in a hot oiled pan for 2 minutes, until translucent. Add curry paste and fry for 1 minute more. Pour in coconut milk, broth, and fish sauce. Stir well until combined. Set heat to medium-high, and add crab meat to the pot. Boil for 3-5 minutes.

While the crab is boiling, cook noodles according to the manufacturer's directions in another pot. Drain and rinse, set aside.

Add shrimp to the broth and boil for 2-3 minutes, until cooked. Add salt and pepper.

Divide broth, noodles, and seafood into separate bowls. Top each bowl with egg halves and chopped cilantro and green onions.

Instant Pot Curry Ramen

Preparation time:	Cooking time:	Servings:
10 minutes	20 minutes	3

Ingredients

- 2 lbs. pork shoulder
- 1 tablespoon soy sauce
- 2 tablespoons lime juice
- 1/4 cup coconut sugar
- 2 tablespoons fish sauce
- 1 teaspoon ginger paste
- 2 garlic cloves, minced
- 4 cups chicken broth
- 2 heads Bok choy, halved
- 1 can full-fat coconut milk
- 3 tablespoons red curry paste
- 1 tablespoon peanut butter
- 14 oz. ramen noodles
- 1 cup fresh cilantro, chopped
- 1/2 cup peanuts, crushed

Directions

Heat the over medium-high and add pork. Cook for 3-4 minutes on each side, until there is a browned crust. After it's done, place pork in the inner pot on top of the steamer grate. Pour fish sauce over the pork, then add garlic and ginger.

Add water that can cover the bottom of the insert.

Set to 60 minutes on high pressure. Do a natural release.

Remove pork and let it cool enough to touch. Leave the liquids in the pot. Transfer pork to a parchment paper-lined baking sheet and shred it into chunks. Drizzle with soy sauce, lime juice, and coconut sugar. Toss to coat pork evenly.

Broil for 5 minutes to caramelize pork on the outside on each side. Remove once all sides get caramelized.

Add coconut milk, chicken broth, peanut butter, and red curry paste to the liquid in the inner pot. Set to Sauté (normal) and bring to a simmer. Cook for 5 minutes, stirring until smooth.

Meanwhile, boil noodles according to the recipe or package instructions.

Build your bowls by adding noodles, broth, caramelized pork, fresh cilantro, and peanuts.

Shrimp Gyoza

Preparation time:	Cooking time:	Servings:
10 minutes	20 minutes	3

Ingredients

- 1 cup cabbage, shredded and finely chopped
- 1/4 teaspoon salt
- 4 stalks scallions, finely chopped
- 2 cloves garlic, peeled and minced
- 1/2 lb. shrimp, peeled, deveined, and chopped
- 1 tablespoon dried baby shrimp
- 1/2 teaspoon soy sauce
- 1 teaspoon sesame oil
- 1/2 teaspoon sugar
- 1/2 tablespoon potato starch
- 1/4 teaspoon salt
- 1/4 teaspoon black pepper
- 18-20 2-inch wonton wrappers
- 1 tablespoon neutral oil
- 1/4 cup water
- Preferred sauce for dipping

Directions

Mix cabbage and 1/2 teaspoon salt in a bowl and toss. Let it sit for 15 minutes.

Squeeze excess liquid from cabbage, then return it to the bowl.

Add garlic, scallions, shrimp, sesame oil, soy sauce, sugar, starch, salt, and pepper, and mix well. Set aside.

Place wonton wrappers on a work surface. Scoop out 1 tablespoon filling and arrange it in the center of each wrapper. Dip fingers in water and run over the edges of each wrapper.

Fold wrappers over the shrimp filling in half-moon shapes and pinch the edges to seal.

Add oil to a large pan over high heat. Once hot, place dumplings in one layer. Fry them in batches.

Fry dumplings for 1 minute and add 1/2 cup water. Shake the pan a little and cover.

Cook for 5-6 minutes, until the bottoms of the dumplings are crispy and golden brown and water has evaporated. Remove from heat.

Serve with preferable sauce.

Beef and Orange Stir Fry

Preparation time:	Cooking time:	Servings:
10 minutes	20 minutes	3

Ingredients

- 100 grams Soba noodles
- 200 grams broccoli
- 4 teaspoon groundnut oil
- 400 grams undercut beef
- 2 teaspoons of Cornflour
- 2 red peppers
- 1 teaspoon ginger
- 4 garlic cloves
- 1 red chili
- 4 spring onions
- 2 oranges
- 1.5 tablespoons honey
- 1 tablespoon rice vinegar
- 1 tablespoon soya sauce

Directions

Boil the soba noodles, drain, and set aside.

Steam the broccoli until it is tender.

Toss the beef slices into corn flour.

Heat 2 teaspoons of groundnut oil in a pan and fry the beef pieces.

In another pan, heat the remaining oil and fry the red peppers.

Add the ginger, garlic, chili, and spring onions and fry for a few minutes.

Now add the orange juice, honey, rice vinegar, and the soya sauce and mix.

Now add in the steamed broccoli, soba noodles, and fried beef.

Garnish with spring onions and serve!

Chili Beef with Broccoli, Egg, Noodles, and Oyster Sauce

Preparation time:	Cooking time:	Servings:
10 minutes	20 minutes	3

Ingredients

- 8 ounces egg noodles
- 500 grams beef undercut
- 2 tablespoons soya sauce
- A pinch of five-spice powder
- 2 tablespoons rice wine
- 1 red chili
- 2 tablespoons cornflour
- 3 tablespoons sunflower oil
- 2 peppers
- 150 grams broccoli
- 200 ml chicken stock
- 2 tablespoons oyster sauce

Directions:

Boil the egg noodles in water, drain and set aside.

Marinate the undercut beef with soya sauce, five-spice powder, rice wine, red chili, and cornflour.

Add sunflower oil into a pan and stir fry the beef.

Take out the beef and heat the pan with oil again.

Stir fry the peppers and the broccoli until they become crispy.

Add in the chicken stock and the oyster sauce.

Now add the beef and let simmer.

Serve with noodles!

Beef, Noodle, and Noodle Stir Fry

Preparation time:	Cooking time:	Servings:
10 minutes	20 minutes	3

Ingredients

- 6 oz. rice noodles

- 3 tablespoons soya sauce

- 2 tablespoons lemon juice

- 2 teaspoons honey

- 1 teaspoon cornstarch

- 1 tablespoon ginger

- 2 tablespoons oil

- 3 stalks of celery

- 2 bell peppers

- 2 garlic cloves

- 1 can water chestnuts

- 1 lb. sirloin steak

- A pinch of black pepper

- 1 cup edamame

- ¼ cup water

Directions

Cook noodles according to the instructions on the package.

In a bowl add the soya sauce, lemon juice, honey, cornstarch, and ¼ cup of water.

Add in the ginger.

Heat oil in a pan and stir fry the celery and the peppers.

Add in the garlic and the chestnuts and fry.

Heat oil in another pan and add in the sirloin steak, season with black pepper.

Add the soya sauce mixture.

Let it cook.

Add in the edamame and the bell peppers and let cook for a few minutes.

Serve with rice noodles!

German Spaghettini

Preparation time:	Cooking time:	Servings:
10 minutes	20 minutes	3

Ingredients

- 1 pound beef
- ¼ cup Italian sausage
- 6 bacon slices
- 15 ounces tomato sauce
- 28 ounces canned tomatoes
- 1/3 cup sugar
- 12 ounces spaghettini
- 2 tablespoons oil

Directions

Boil the spaghettini in a large saucepan filled with water.

Drain and set aside.

Add oil into a frying pan and fry the ground beef until it is cooked.

Remove from heat and now fry the sausage in the frying pan.

Now add in the cooked beef.

Add in the bacon slices, tomato sauce, tomatoes, and canned tomatoes.

Let it cook for 40 minutes.

Now mix in the cooked Spaghettini in the tomato mixture.

Pour this in a baking rectangular dish.

Preheat your oven to 300 degrees Fahrenheit.

Put this baking dish in the preheated oven to bake for 30 minutes.

Serve!

Chapter 5: Anytime Boards

Chunky Chili-con-Carne

Preparation time:	Cooking time:	Servings:
10 minutes	50 minutes	4

Ingredients

- 1 pound of ground beef
- 1 onion
- 1 tablespoon of sunflower oil
- 1 3/4 cup of chopped tomatoes (14-ounce can)
- 2 garlic cloves
- 1 red pepper
- 1/8 teaspoon of salt
- 1/8 teaspoon of pepper
- 2 teaspoons of chili powder
- 1 teaspoon of oregano
- 1 teaspoon of cumin, ground
- 1 3/4 cup of kidney beans (14-ounce can)
- 1 cup of beef broth
- 2 tablespoons of tomato puree
- 1 cube of dark chocolate

Directions

To prepare for freezing:

Place a large skillet on the stove, and set the temperature to medium heat.

Pour the oil into the pan, and heat.

Add the ground beef, and season with salt and black pepper.

Cook the beef until it is golden brown, about 15 minutes.

Drain, but keep the oil, and place it in a large bowl. Allow to cool.

Return the skillet to the stove, and add the oil you drained off.

Mince the garlic, and stir it into the oil.

Whisk together the cumin, chili powder, and oregano. Add the garlic in the pan.

Sauté for a minute or until the spices become fragrant.

Fold in the tomato purée

Add the tomatoes with their juice.

Whisk in the broth.

Bring the mixture to a boil, and then pour over the meat. Mix well.

Wash, peel, and chop the onion. Add to the meat mixture.

Wash, seed, and thinly slice the red pepper, then fold it into the meat.

Mix well before pouring into a freezer bag.

Seal and label the bag with the date you prepared the meal as well as the cooking time and heat setting.

Freeze.

To slow cook:

To cook, take it out of the freezer.

Place the ingredients of the bag into the slow cooker.

Turn the slow cooker to low, and cook for 7 hours.

After the time has passed, rinse the kidney beans, and drain them.

Stir into the meat mixture, and continue cooking for another hour.

When it is done, place the chocolate cube into the chili, and stir well until it is melted.

Serve warm.

Hungry Man Stew

Preparation time:	Cooking time:	Servings:
10 minutes	60 minutes	4

Ingredients

- 1 pound ground beef

- 1 medium onion, sliced

- 1 tablespoon cooking oil

- 2 cups carrots, diced

- 3 russet potatoes, diced

- 1 16-ounce can kidney beans, drained

- ¼ cup uncooked long grain rice

- 1 8-ounce can tomato sauce

- 4 cups water

- ¼ teaspoon chili powder

- ¼ cup Worcestershire sauce

- Non-stick cooking spray

Directions

Coat the slow cooker with non-stick cooking spray.

In a skillet, heat the oil and brown the meat and onion. Drain off the grease and transfer meat to a slow cooker.

Add the carrots, potatoes, kidney beans, rice, tomato sauce, water, chili powder, and Worcestershire sauce.

Cover and cook for 6-8 hours on LOW. If the potatoes and rice are still too firm after 6 hours of cooking, continue cooking for another hour, and then check every 30 minutes or so for doneness.

Pioneer Goulash

Preparation time: 10 minutes

Cooking time: 30 minutes

Servings: 5

Ingredients

- 1 pound ground beef

- 1 cup yellow onion, diced

- ½ cup celery, chopped

- 1 tablespoon jarred minced garlic

- 1 15-ounce can diced tomatoes

- 1 15-ounce can tomato sauce

- 1 15-ounce can kidney beans, drained

- 1½ cups water or tomato-based vegetable juice

- 1 tablespoon Worcestershire sauce

- 1 tablespoon soy sauce

- 1 teaspoon oregano

- 1 teaspoon thyme

- 1 teaspoon paprika

- 1 teaspoon salt

- 1 teaspoon pepper

- 1-2 cups uncooked elbow macaroni

Directions

Prepare the Dutch oven by heating the coals and placing the oven on top of them.

Once the oven is heated, add the ground beef, onion, celery, and garlic. Toss while cooking just until meat is browned, approximately 10 minutes.

Add the tomatoes, tomato sauce, kidney beans, vegetable juice, Worcestershire sauce, and soy sauce. Cover and continue cooking until the liquid becomes hot and bubbly.

Season with oregano, thyme, paprika, salt, and pepper. Continue to simmer for 5 minutes.

Add the elbow macaroni, cover, and continue cooking for 30 minutes or until pasta is tender.

Beef Chili

Preparation time:	Cooking time:	Servings:
10 minutes	30 minutes	4

Ingredients

- 1 ¼ pounds lean ground beef

- 3 tablespoons grass-fed ghee

- 1 carrot, chopped

- 2 celery stalks, finely chopped

- 4 tomatoes, chopped

- ½ teaspoon cumin seeds, ground

- 1 teaspoon oregano

- ½ teaspoon cinnamon

- 1 teaspoon sea salt

- 3 cups Bok choy, chopped

- 1 avocado, pitted and peeled

Directions

Heat 3 tablespoons of grass-fed ghee in a soup pot over medium heat, add beef and brown.

Add the carrot, celery, tomatoes, cumin, oregano, cinnamon, and salt, and cook for 30 minutes.

Add the Bok choy and avocado, and cook for 10 more minutes, until the Bok choy is wilted and the avocado is heated through.

Classic Beef Chili

Preparation time:	Cooking time:	Servings:
10 minutes	30 minutes	4

Ingredients

- 3 tablespoons butter
- 1 pound of lean ground beef
- Salt and pepper to taste
- 1 teaspoon Dijon mustard
- 1 spring onion, finely chopped
- 1 clove garlic, minced
- 1 teaspoon paprika
- 1 teaspoon dried oregano
- 1 red chili, diced
- 1 (16-ounce) can of red kidney beans
- 2 cups tomato sauce
- 1 cup beef stock
- 2 tablespoons freshly chopped basil
- 2 tablespoons freshly chopped parsley

Directions

Warm the beef stock and add the ground beef.

Season with salt and pepper, Dijon mustard, spring onion, garlic, oregano and paprika, and chili.

Cook for 5 minutes, then stir in the beans, tomato sauce, and beef stock.

Cook for 20 minutes. Sprinkle with parsley and basil and cook for 10 more minutes.

Beef Cheesy Chili

Preparation time:	Cooking time:	Servings:
10 minutes	50 minutes	4

Ingredients

- 3 tablespoons olive oil
- 1 pound of lean ground beef
- Salt and pepper to taste
- 1 teaspoon tomato paste
- 1 teaspoon onion powder
- 1 clove garlic, minced
- 1 teaspoon paprika
- 1 teaspoon dried oregano
- 1 red chili, diced
- 1 (16-ounce) can sweet corn
- 2 cups tomato sauce
- 1 cup beef stock
- 2 tablespoons freshly chopped parsley
- 1 cup grated cheddar cheese

Directions

Heat olive oil in a pan

Add the ground beef.

Season with salt and pepper, tomato paste, onion powder, garlic, oregano and paprika, and chili.

Cook for 5 minutes and stir in the corn, tomato sauce, and beef stock.

Cook for another 20 minutes.

Sprinkle in the parsley and cook for 10 more minutes.

Just before serving, sprinkle the grated cheddar cheese on top.

Slow Cooker Simple Cheesy Chili Recipe

Preparation time:	Cooking time:	Servings:
10 minutes	50 minutes	4

Ingredients

- 1 pound ground beef, browned, drained

- 2 packets chili seasoning

- 2 cans (14½ ounces each) tomatoes with chipotle chilies, diced

- ¾ pound elbow macaroni

- Cheese, grated and sour cream (optional)

Directions

Mix the first three ingredients in your slow cooker.

Cook on low heat for 8 hours.

When the beef is almost done, cook the pasta and add it to the crockpot.

Let everything cook for another half hour.

Transfer everything to a bowl or plate, top with the optional ingredients (if desired), and serve.

Garlic and Spice Beef Chili

Preparation time:	Cooking time:	Servings:
10 minutes	30 minutes	4

Ingredients

- 1 pound of lean beef, browned
- 1 cup onion, diced
- 6 cloves garlic, crushed and minced
- 2 jalapeño peppers, sliced
- ½ cup tomato paste
- 2 cups stewed tomatoes, with liquid
- ¼ cup canned green chilies
- 1 cup tomato juice
- ¼ cup chili powder
- 1 tablespoon ground cumin
- 2 teaspoons cocoa powder
- 1 teaspoon mustard powder
- 1 teaspoon onion powder
- 1 teaspoon salt
- 1 teaspoon black pepper
- 1 teaspoon oregano
- ½ cup sour cream
- 1 avocado, sliced
- ¼ cup fresh cilantro

Directions

Top the ground beef with onion, garlic, jalapeno peppers, tomato paste, stewed tomatoes, green chilies, and tomato juice. Mix well,

Next, season the chili with chili powder, cumin, cocoa powder, mustard, onion powder, salt, black pepper, and oregano. Mix again.

Serve the chili garnished with sour cream, avocado, and fresh cilantro.

Mom's Chili

Preparation time:	Cooking time:	Servings:
10 minutes	30 minutes	4

Ingredients

- 2 pounds of ground beef, lean
- 2 medium cooking onions
- 6 garlic cloves
- 1 red bell pepper
- 1/4 cup of pickled jalapenos
- 3 3/4 cups of kidney beans (2 15-ounce cans)
- 3 1/2 cups of diced tomatoes (1 28 ounce can)
- 1 3/4 cups of tomato sauce (1 14 ounce can)
- 3 tablespoons of vegetable oil
- 1/4 cup of chili powder
- 1 tablespoon of cumin
- 1 1/2 teaspoons of salt
- Garnish (optional)
- 1 cup of cheddar cheese, shredded
- 1/4 cup of sliced scallions
- 1 cup of sour cream

Directions

To prepare for freezing:

Heat until it is bubbling.

Wash, peel, and chop the onions.

Wash, seed, and chop the bell pepper.

Place the onions and bell pepper into the hot oil.

Fry until the vegetables are soft, usually between 5 to 8 minutes.

Mince the garlic, and add to the pan.

Mix in the chili powder and cumin, and stir until all the ingredients are coated in the spices. Continue to cook for another minute.

Once you can smell the spices, add the ground beef and the salt to the frying pan. Cook until the ground beef is brown, about 7 to 10 minutes.

When cooked, remove from heat and cool completely.

In a large bowl, mix the diced tomatoes, with their juice, and tomato sauce.

Drain and rinse the kidney beans. Add to the tomatoes.

Chop the jalapenos and add to the tomatoes.

Stir until the ingredients are blended thoroughly.

Fold in the cooled beef mixture. Stir until the meat is coated.

Transfer to a freezer bag.

Seal and label the freezer bag with the name of the dish, the date you prepared the meal, the cooking time, and the heat setting. Freeze.

To slow cook:

Remove the bag from the freezer, and pour the ingredients into a slow cooker.

Set the temperature to low, and allow it to cook for 6 hours.

If you like, garnish with cheese, scallions, or sour cream. Serve warm.

Nutrition: Calories 540, Fat 10.5 g, Fiber 9.6 g, Carbs 51.6 g, Protein 11.4 g

Classic Chili Con Carne

Preparation time:	Cooking time:	Servings:
10 minutes	60 minutes	4

Ingredients

- 1½-2 pounds lean ground beef

- 1 onion, diced

- 1 green bell pepper, trimmed and diced

- 2 cans low-sodium diced tomatoes

- 1 can red kidney beans

- 2 garlic cloves, minced

- 1-2 tablespoons vegetable oil

- 2-3 tablespoons make-ahead chili spice mix (recipe below)

- Tex-Mex shredded cheese for topping

Directions

Heat 1-2 tablespoons of oil in a large iron cast saucepan (or a Dutch oven) set on the grill over the campfire or on a camping propane/gas barbecue set on medium-high heat. Add the diced onions and garlic, and cook for 1-2 minutes until they are tender and fragrant. Add the ground beef and stir-fry until the meat is cooked through, about 5-10 minutes. Remove from heat.

Add diced green peppers, tomatoes, and chili spices. Give it a few stirs, cover with the lid, and place directly on the white coals. Let it cook for 1 hour before adding the red kidney beans. Cook for an additional 30-45 minutes.

Serve in bowls and top with shredded cheese.

Nutrition: Calories 190, Fat 8.1, Fiber 5.8, Carbs 11.6, Protein 4.6

Chili Con Carne I

Preparation time: 10 minutes

Cooking time: 50 minutes

Servings: 4

Nutrition: Calories 278, Fat 7.3, Fiber 6.8, Carbs 38.1, Protein 16.3

Ingredients

- 1 10½ ounce can hot-style vegetable juice
- 1 15½ ounce can diced tomatoes
- 3 green chilies, undrained
- 1 pound ground beef
- 1 large onion, diced
- 15½ ounces water

Directions

On the stove, heat a skillet coated with cooking spray. Cook onions until the meat is tender and brown. Add ground beef, and continue cooking until the meat is well cooked.

Place the ground beef mixture, undrained tomatoes, beans, green chilies, and vegetable juice in the slow cooker.

Add a full can of water using the diced tomato can. Stir and cover.

Cook on low heat for 6-7 hours.

Chili Con Carne II

Preparation time:	Cooking time:	Servings:
10 minutes	2 hours	4

Ingredients

- 5 ½ cups of water

- 5 teaspoons of salt, divided

- 3 pounds of lean ground beef

- 1 ½ cups of chopped onions

- 1 cup of chopped bell peppers

- 1 teaspoon of black pepper

- 3-6 teaspoons of chili powder, to taste

- 2 cans crushed tomatoes, 28 ounces each

Directions

Wash kidney beans, and put them into a 2-quart saucepan. Top the beans with cold water about 2-3 above the beans, and let the beans soak for a good twelve to 15 hours.

Drain the water, mix the beans with 5 ½ cups of cold water with the 2 teaspoons of salt, and let it boil.

Reduce the heat, let it cook30 minutes, drain, and reserve.

Brown the ground beef with chopped onions and optional peppers in a skillet. Drain off the fat, and add salt, pepper, tomatoes, chili powder, and beans.

Let simmer for about 5 minutes, and then put into jars. Pressure cook at 10 pounds for 2 hours for the weighted gauge of the pressure canner or 11 pounds if the pressure canner has a dial gauge.

Remove jars, and let them cool completely at room temperature before storing. This can take about a day.

Hakata Tonkotsu Ramen

Preparation time:	Cooking time:	Servings:
10 minutes	40 minutes	3

Ingredients

For the broth:

- 2 pig trotters, cleaned well

- 1 big white onion, finely diced

- 1/4 cup oil

- 5 cloves garlic, crushed

- 5 cm fresh ginger, crushed

- 6 cups water

- For the ramen:

- 1 tablespoon oil

- 2 cloves finely grated garlic

- 1 teaspoon salt

- 1 teaspoon mirin

- 3 slices boiled char siu

- 2 teaspoons dried wakame

- 10-15 strips of kombu

- 1 portion ramen noodles

- For the toppings:

- 1 Nitamago egg

- 1 stock spring onion, finely chopped

- 1 teaspoon toasted white sesame seeds

- 2 teaspoons of Mayu

- 1 slice toasted seaweed

- Pickled red ginger, as needed

Directions

Bring a pot of hot water to a boil, then add pig trotters and cook for 15 minutes in boiling water. Discard water and clean the pot thoroughly. Cut open pig trotters a little in a basin of cold water, and let out as much blood as possible. Repeat this step 3 times, until water is clear of blood and other impurities.

Bring a large pot of water to boil, and add pig trotters. Reduce heat to medium and let simmer.

Meanwhile, heat some oil in a pan. Stir ginger and garlic for 30 seconds. Add them to the stock.

With the same oil in the pan, stir fry the onion until brown and caramelized. Add to the stock.

Cover and simmer the stock for 6 hours on low heat, until the trotters open up completely and the soup is rich, sticky, and thick. Strain it through a fine strainer. The soup base is ready.

Heat oil and sauté garlic in a pot. Add 3 ladles of soup base and bring to a boil.

Add 3 slices of skinny pork belly, dried wakame, kombu, mirin, and salt and pepper to taste.

In another pot, cook ramen noodles. Drain and serve in a bowl.

Pour soup into the bowl. Top with boiled pork, spring onions, Mayu, toasted sesame seeds, sliced pickled red ginger, seaweed, and nitamago egg.

Tokyo Ramen

Preparation time:	Cooking time:	Servings:
10 minutes	40 minutes	3

Ingredients

- 2 portions ramen noodles

- 2 cups chicken stock

- 2 tablespoons shoyu soy sauce

- Spinach, to taste

- Nori, to taste

- 1 bunch green onion, chopped if desired

- 1/4 cup Dashi

For the Egg:

- 4 eggs

- 1/2 cup soy sauce

- 2 tablespoons brown sugar

- 1/3 cup water

- 3 tablespoons rice vinegar

- 3 tablespoons sliced green onion

- 1 tablespoon sliced ginger

For the toppings:

- Nori, to taste

- Chopped green onion, to taste

Directions

Mix soy sauce, brown sugar, water, and rice vinegar in a small bowl. Add ginger and green onion, mix again. Set aside until ready to use.

Pour 4 cups of water into a small pot and bring to a boil. Add 4 eggs and lower heat to medium. Cook for 7 minutes uncovered. Transfer eggs to ice water. Cool for 5 minutes and then peel.

Put eggs in the soy sauce mixture and cover with plastic wrap. Be sure the eggs are completely covered with marinade. Put in the fridge for 4-8 hours, depending on desired saltiness.

Preheat the oven to 300°F.

Heat oil in a frying pan over medium heat. Add pork belly fat side down. Cook until golden brown, 4 minutes per side. Transfer pork belly (fat side down) to a deep baking dish.

Add soy sauce, sake, water, honey, garlic, ginger, and green onions to the dish with pork belly. Toss everything together until all ingredients are well mixed.

Bake for 3 hours, flipping the meat halfway through.

Remove from the oven and let cool in the brine. Cover and refrigerate overnight.

Slice the pork belly into 1-inch-thick pieces.

Cut the eggs in half.

Pour 2 cups of water into a pot and bring to a boil. Add ramen noodles and stir for 2 minutes until cooked. Take out noodles and assemble in bowls.

Blanch some spinach in the same water and add to bowls.

Heat 2 cups of chicken stock in another pot and add dashi to it. Bring to a boil.

Add shoyu soy sauce and chicken stock to each bowl.

Place ramen into a bowl and top with sliced pork, marinated eggs, and menma.

Thai Shrimp Noodle Soup

Preparation time:	Cooking time:	Servings:
10 minutes	40 minutes	5

Ingredients

- 3 tablespoons peeled and very thinly slivered fresh ginger

- 10 oz. medium-size shrimp, peeled and deveined

- 2 ½ tablespoons fish sauce or soy sauce

- 3 carrots, thinly sliced

- 2 cloves garlic, finely minced

- 2 teaspoon chopped fresh basil

- 3 cups coarsely chopped fresh spinach

- 10 cups water

- 3 packets of chicken flavored Ramen noodles

- 4 green onions, minced

- 2 tablespoons Thai hot chili sauce

- 1 cup sliced mushrooms

- Juice and grated zest from 1 ½ lime

Instructions

Fill a large pot with water. Bring this water to a boil on a high flame.

Add the carrots, fish sauce, green onions, ginger, garlic, basil, and chili sauce.

Break the noodles and put them into the water as well. Keep stirring to separate the strands.

Now add the seasoning from 2 packets that came with the noodles. Boil for 5 minutes or so.

After this, add the shrimp, mushrooms, and spinach. Cook for another 5 minutes.

Top with lime zest and juice and stir well.

Cranberry Nectarine Salad

Preparation time:	Cooking time:	Servings:
5 minutes	20 minutes	3

Ingredients

- Two 3 oz. packets of Ramen noodles
- 1 ½ tablespoon soy sauce
- 1 packet of gourmet mixed salad greens (wash them thoroughly)
- 2 tablespoons light brown sugar
- 1 tablespoon balsamic vinegar
- 1 cup dried cranberries
- 2 cups hot water
- ½ cup canola oil
- 1 ½ tablespoon rice wine vinegar
- 2 large nectarines, peeled and cut in wedges
- 1 cup coarsely chopped walnuts
- 10 oz. crumbled feta cheese

Directions

Preheat the oven to 350 degrees Fahrenheit.

Keep the packets of seasoning that come with the soup mix aside. Break the noodles into smaller pieces and place them in a pan. Make sure that they are as spread out as possible.

Put this pan in the oven. Bake at the same temperature for around 6 minutes. Remove the pan when the noodles are toasted. Stir them occasionally so that the heat is evenly spread out.

After this, place the pan aside to cool the noodles down.

In a small bowl, pour the cranberries. Heat some water (not boil) and add this to the cranberries. Leave the cranberries in the water for some time and then drain the water.

In another large bowl, whisk the contents from the seasoning packet with the canola oil and the four ingredients that follow from the list above.

Add the cranberries, gourmet greens, Ramen noodles, and the rest of the ingredients to this bowl. Toss the contents to mix well. Serve when hot.

Kurume Ramen

Preparation time:	Cooking time:	Servings:
10 minutes	40 minutes	3

Ingredients

For the broth:

- 4 cups pork broth

- 2 tablespoons mirin

- 1 tablespoon of sake

- Salt, to taste

- 1 tablespoon chili oil, if desired

For the ramen:

- 0.5 lb. Cha Shu pork, sliced

- 4 nori sheets

- 1 green onion, sliced

- 1/4 cup bamboo shoots

- 2 portions ramen noodles

- 2 halved ramen eggs

- Beni-shoga, to taste

Directions

Mix broth, mirin, and salt in a pot. Simmer for 10 minutes on medium-low.

Boil noodles according to the package in another pot. Drain, and divide between 2 bowls.

Add broth to the bowls. Top with bamboo shoots, pork, eggs, beni-shoga, scallions, and nori.

Serve with chili oil.

Tsukemen Ramen

Preparation time:	Cooking time:	Servings:
10 minutes	40 minutes	3

Ingredients

For the ramen:

- 2 servings ramen noodles

- 1/2 lb. sliced pork belly, cut into 1-inch pieces

- ½ inch ginger, minced

- 3 cloves garlic, minced

- 2 shiitake mushrooms, sliced

- 1/2 shimeji mushrooms, sliced

- 2 green onions/scallions, chopped

- 1 tablespoon sesame oil

- 1 tablespoon spicy chili bean sauce or broad bean paste

- 1 package dried bonito flakes

For the seasonings:

- 1/3 cup Mentsuyu

- 1 cup water

- 1 teaspoon miso

- 1 teaspoon soy sauce

- 1 1/2 tablespoons rice vinegar

- For the toppings:

- 1 tablespoon of sake

- 2 soft/hard-boiled egg

- 2-3 slices Narutomaki

- Nori sheet

Directions

Heat sesame oil in a saucepan over medium-high heat.

Once hot, add ginger and garlic and cook for 30 seconds. Add chili bean paste and stir constantly to avoid burning it. Next, add meat and cook for 3-4 minutes, or until no longer pink. Add shimeji mushrooms and cook until wilted.

Pour in Mentsuyu and water and bring to a boil.

Skim off the scum and foam with a fine sieve if necessary.

Reduce heat to medium-low, add miso and soy sauce, and simmer for 5 minutes.

Add green onions and rice vinegar. Turn off heat and set aside.

Prepare all the toppings, then bring a large pot of water to a boil and cook noodles, following directions in the recipe or on the package. Drain and rinse the noodles to remove starch. Place noodles in a bowl of ice water and soak to cool. Drain and divide into bowls. Serve noodles with all toppings.

Pour the hot soup in separate bowls, sprinkle with bonito flakes and serve alongside cold noodles and toppings.

Kitakata Ramen

Preparation time:	Cooking time:	Servings:
10 minutes	40 minutes	3

Ingredients

For the ramen:

- 3 cups pork broth
- 2 tablespoons soy sauce
- 11/2 tablespoons mirin
- 2 tablespoons dried sardines
- 2 servings noodles

For the toppings:

- 1/2 lbs. pork belly
- 1/2 cup menma
- 1/2 cup scallions
- 4 slices Naruto fish cake

Directions

Heat pork broth in a pot and add soy sauce, mirin, and dried sardines. Bring to a simmer and cook for 15 minutes, until you prepare other toppings.

Bring another pot of water to boil and cook noodles. Boil for 12 minutes, or follow directions on the package, stirring occasionally. Strain noodles and portion into bowls.

While noodles are boiling, prepare the toppings. Slice fish cake and pork belly into thin slices, chop the scallions.

Strain sardines from the broth and pour them into bowls. Add noodles and toppings, then serve!

Sesame Noodles

Preparation time: **Cooking time:** **Servings:**

10 minutes 40 minutes 5

Ingredients

- 16 ounces spaghetti
- 6 garlic cloves
- 6 tablespoons sugar
- 6 tablespoons safflower oil
- 6 tablespoons rice vinegar
- 6 tablespoons soya sauce
- 2 tablespoons sesame oil
- 2 teaspoons chili sauce
- 6 green onions
- 1 teaspoon toasted sesame seeds
- 4 cups water

Directions

Add water to a large pot and add the pasta to boil.

Add salt.

Drain and set aside once done.

Heat safflower oil in a frying pan and add in the garlic, sugar, sesame oil, rice vinegar, soya sauce, and chili sauce.

Stir until dissolved.

Pour this prepared sauce over the cooked spaghetti.

Cut the green onions and mix in.

Toast the sesame seeds and sprinkle them over the cooked pasta.

Serve!

Noodles with Butter

Ingredients

- 16 ounces fettuccine noodles

- 6 tablespoons butter

- 1/3 cup grated parmesan cheese

- A pinch of salt

- A pinch of pepper

- 4 cups water

Directions

Fill a large pot with water and add in the salt.

Add in the fettuccini noodles and boil them.

Drain and set aside once boiled.

Add the pasta into an empty pot.

Now mix in the butter, salt, pepper, and grated parmesan cheese.

Mix and serve!

Salmon Miso Ramen

Preparation time:	Cooking time:	Servings:
10 minutes	40 minutes	5

Ingredients

- 6 oz. of udon noodles

- 2½ cups of water

- Dashi

- 2 tablespoons of miso paste

- 3.5 oz. of salmon fillet

- 3.5 oz. of tofu (in small cubes)

- 2 spring onions (cut into rings)

- 10 sheets of wakame

- 6 shiitake mushrooms (dried, cut into fine strips)

- 1 tablespoon of chives

- Soy sauce

- 1 egg (whisked)

Instructions

Heat the water with dashi in a larger saucepan. Add the tofu cubes and shiitake strips. Let cook for about 10 minutes. Add the onions and let simmer for another 5 minutes. Add salmon fillet strips and the whisked egg as desired, cook for 2-3 minutes.

Stir in the miso paste with a little soup and add cooked noodles and wakame leaves to the soup, boil it again. Season to taste and serve sprinkled with chives.

Fish stock can also be used instead of water and dashi since it is a soy-based fish soup.

The individual toppings can be varied or left out. With all the trimmings, you get a stew that goes as the main course. Serve with tofu, shiitake, spring onions, egg, and/or wakame.

Fast Miso Ramen

Preparation time:	Cooking time:	Servings:
10 minutes	40 minutes	5

Ingredients

- 6 oz. of noodles
- 2 tablespoons of miso paste
- 2 cloves of garlic
- 1 tablespoon of sambal oelek
- 2½ cups of vegetable broth
- 2 oz. of mung bean sprouts
- 4 small discs of roast pork (cooked)
- 4 surimi pieces
- 1 oz. of corn
- 2 seaweed leaves
- 2 spring onions
- Vegetable oil

Instructions

Cook the ramen noodles.

Heat the oil in the saucepan. Add garlic and sambal oelek. Before it turns brown, add the broth and stir in the miso paste.

Rinse the mung bean seedlings with water and put them briefly in the broth, as well as the roast pork and the surimi pieces, so that they become warm.

Cut the spring onions into small pieces.

Place the noodles in a large bowl. Arrange everything in a circle except the spring onions. Pour in the broth from the center (let it get really hot again beforehand). Finally, put the spring onions in the middle.

Asian Shrimp and Noodle Soup

Preparation time:	Cooking time:	Servings:
10 minutes	40 minutes	3

Ingredients:

- 9 cups water

- 3 ramen noodle packets

- 10 oz. frozen, cooked, peeled, and deveined medium shrimp

- 2 teaspoons dark oriental sesame oil

- ½ teaspoon crushed red pepper.

- 1 cup chopped scallions

- ½ cup grated carrots

Instructions

Take a clean and dry pot and add the water to it. Bring this up to a boil.

Now break the blocks of noodles into 4 pieces each and add them to the pot.

Cook for around 5 minutes while constantly stirring. This will ensure that the strands separate from each other. Cook until the noodles are tender.

Take the pot off the heat now. Add the shrimp and the packets of seasoning to the pot immediately. Also, add the oil and the crushed peppers.

Let cool for around 2 minutes. Sprinkle the scallions and carrots over the top. You may grate some cheese over the top if you want to.

Serve hot with lime wedges.

Dad's Favorite Casserole

Preparation time:	Cooking time:	Servings:
10 minutes	20 minutes	3

Ingredients

- 1 pound ground beef
- 1 clove garlic, minced
- salt and pepper to taste
- 1 (10 ounces) package frozen chopped spinach, thawed and drained
- 1 (16 ounces) package uncooked wide egg noodles
- 1 (10.75 ounces) can of condensed cream of mushroom soup
- 2 1/2 cups fat-free milk
- 1 cup shredded American cheese

Direction

Preheat the oven to 325°F (165°C). Coat a big casserole dish with a little bit of oil.

Put the ground beef in a skillet and let it cook on medium heat until the ground beef is browned evenly. Drain off the beef grease. Add in the garlic and put in pepper and salt to taste. Mix in the spinach and let it cook until thoroughly heated. Add in the uncooked egg noodles and mix; place the mixture in the greased casserole dish. Put in the milk and cream of mushroom soup then mix and top it off with cheese.

Put it in a preheated oven and let it bake for 45 minutes until the mixture is bubbling.

Beef and Water Spinach Noodles

Preparation time:	Cooking time:	Servings:
10 minutes	20 minutes	3

Ingredients

- 7 oz. beef (scotch fillet or rump)
- 1 tablespoon cornstarch
- 3 tablespoon soy sauce
- 1 teaspoon sugar
- 1 teaspoon rice wine, or dry sherry
- 4 tablespoon peanut oil
- 10 oz. dried wheat noodles
- 14 oz. water spinach (Ong Choy), thoroughly washed
- 2 spring onions, finely sliced
- 1 tablespoon ginger, grated
- 2 cloves of garlic, finely chopped
- 1 tablespoon hoisin sauce
- 2 tablespoons chicken stock
- ½ teaspoon salt
- Pinch of black pepper

Instructions

Finely slice meat into thin strips 2 in long. Rub cornstarch into the meat, combine with 1 tablespoon soy sauce, sugar, rice wine, and 1 tablespoon oil, and leave to marinate for an hour

Cook noodles in plenty of salted, boiling water for about 4 minutes, or until tender, then rinse well under cold water, drain and set aside.

Cut water spinach into 6 in. (2½ in.) pieces.

Heat 2 teaspoons of oil in a hot wok and stir fry water spinach for a minute or two, moving continuously. Remove spinach, set aside, and add 1 more tablespoon of oil to the wok. Stir fry beef for 1 minute, add half the spring onion, the ginger, garlic, and hoisin sauce, and stir fry for another minute over high heat. Add remaining 2 tablespoons soy sauce, stock, salt, and black pepper. When the liquid starts to boil, add the noodles and water spinach and heat through, stirring well to combine. Sprinkle with spring onion and serve.

Chapter 6: Special Occasion Boards

Cheesy Ground Beef Salad

Preparation time:	Cooking time:	Servings:
10 minutes	50 minutes	4

Ingredients

- 2 tablespoons butter
- ½ pound lean ground beef
- Salt and pepper to taste
- 1 teaspoon dried basil
- ½ pound iceberg lettuce
- ½ cup cheddar cheese, diced
- ¼ cup grated parmesan cheese
- Dressing
- 3 tablespoons olive oil
- 1 tablespoon Dijon mustard
- ¼ cup mayonnaise
- Salt and pepper to taste
- Zest of 1 lemon
- 2 tablespoons freshly chopped mint

Directions

Heat the oil and add the ground beef.

Season with salt and pepper and basil. Let cool completely.

Arrange the lettuce in a salad bowl and add the cooled ground beef, cheddar, and parmesan.

Mix the olive oil, Dijon mustard, mayonnaise, salt and pepper, lemon peel, and freshly chopped mint in a jar.

Serve.

Nutrition: Calories 340, Fat 20.4, Fiber 6.6, Carbs 22.3, Protein 18.

Deep-Fried Prawn and Rice Croquettes

Preparation time:	Cooking time:	Servings:
10 minutes	40 minutes	5

Ingredients

- 2 tablespoons butter
- 1/2 onion, finely chopped
- 4 ounces peeled shrimp, chopped
- 2 tablespoons all-purpose flour
- 1 tablespoon white wine
- 1/2 cup milk
- 2 tablespoons milk
- 2 cups cooked rice
- 1 tablespoon grated Parmesan cheese, or more to taste
- 1 teaspoon chopped fresh dill, or more to taste
- 1 teaspoon salt
- Ground black pepper
- Vegetable oil for frying
- 3 tablespoons all-purpose flour, or as needed
- 1 egg
- 1/2 cup bread crumbs

Direction

In a big skillet, put the butter and let it melt over medium heat. Put in the onion and cook while stirring it for about 5 minutes until the onion becomes soft and has turned brown. Put in the shrimp and let it cook for 1-2 minutes while stirring it until the shrimp becomes opaque. Add the white wine and 2 tablespoons of flour and mix well. Gradually add the milk and let it cook for 3-5 minutes while continuously stirring using a wooden spoon until the white sauce is thick.

Remove the white sauce mixture away from the heat. Add the rice and give it a mix until evenly blended. Put in the salt, Parmesan cheese, dill, and black pepper. Allow the mixture to cool down for about 15 minutes until it is easy to touch.

Put the oil in a big saucepan or a deep-fryer and let it heat up to 350°F (175°C) temperature.

In a shallow bowl, put 3 tablespoons of flour. In a small bowl, put the egg and beat it. On a plate, put the bread crumbs and spread them out evenly.

Shape the rice mixture into 8 pieces of ball-sized equally. Take 1 ball and roll it in the flour, then dip it in the beaten egg and coat it evenly with bread crumbs. Do the same process for the rest of the rice balls.

Put the rice balls into the preheated deep-fryer and let it deep-fry in the hot oil for about 3 minutes until it turns golden brown.

Marvel's Japanese Fried Oysters (Kaki Fuh Rai) With Lemony Tartar Sauce

Preparation time:	Cooking time:	Servings:
10 minutes	40 minutes	5

Ingredients

- 1 cup mayonnaise

- 1/2 lemon, juiced, and zested

- 1/4 dill pickle spear, seeded and minced

- 1/4 teaspoon cayenne pepper

- 1 cup panko (Japanese bread crumbs)

- 1/8 teaspoon cayenne pepper

- salt and ground black pepper to taste

- 2 cups canola oil

- 6 shucked oysters, or more if desired

- 1 egg, beaten

Direction

For preheating, set the oven at 250 degrees Fahrenheit or 120 degrees Celsius.

Tartar sauce: In a small bowl, stir together 1/4 teaspoon cayenne pepper, dill pickle, lemon zest, lemon juice, and mayonnaise until thoroughly combined, and set aside.

In a shallow bowl, mix black pepper, salt, 1/8 teaspoon cayenne pepper, and panko crumbs.

In a deep-fryer or saucepan, heat canola oil to 360 degrees Fahrenheit or 180 degrees Celsius. For accuracy, measure the temperature with a deep-frying thermometer.

Dip oyster onto the beaten egg and press into the panko mixture to coat. Toss gently between your hands for the bread crumbs that aren't stuck would fall away. Place breaded oysters on a plate while breading the others, but do not stack.

Cook oysters, 2 each time, into hot oil for about 1 minute per side until panko turns brown. Transfer fried oysters onto a baking sheet that is lined with paper towels. Place in the oven to keep warm while you fry the remaining oysters. Serve along with the tartar sauce for dipping.

Orange Ponzu

Preparation time:	Cooking time:	Servings:
10 minutes	40 minutes	5

Ingredients

- 1/4 cup soy sauce

- 1/2 cup rice vinegar

- 2 tablespoons bonito shavings (dry fish flakes)

- 1 (1 inch) square kombu (kelp)

- 1 orange, quartered

Direction

Mix the orange quarters, konbu, bonito shavings, rice vinegar, and soy sauce in a saucepan. Allow to stand for a half-hour.

Bring to a boil. Once it begins to boil, take it away from the heat. Let it cool, then strain a sieve lined with cheesecloth.

Baby Spinach and Ground Beef Salad

Preparation time:	Cooking time:	Servings:
10 minutes	40 minutes	4

Ingredients

- 2 tablespoons butter
- ½ pound ground sirloin
- Salt and pepper to taste
- 1 teaspoon dried dill
- ½ pound baby spinach
- 1 cup diced strawberries
- ¼ cup grated parmesan cheese
- 1 cup mozzarella balls
- Dressing
- 3 tablespoons olive oil
- 1 tablespoon Dijon mustard
- 2 tablespoons balsamic vinegar
- Salt and pepper to taste

Directions

Using a nonstick frying pan, heat the oil. Add the ground beef.

Season with salt and pepper and dill. Let cool completely.

Arrange the baby spinach in a salad bowl and add the cooled ground beef, sliced strawberries, parmesan, and mozzarella balls.

Mix the olive oil, Dijon mustard, balsamic vinegar and salt, and pepper in a jar.

Nutrition: Calories 340, Fat 20.7, Fiber 7, Carbs 28.9, Protein 12.5

Cesar Ground Beef Salad

Preparation time:	Cooking time:	Servings:
10 minutes	40 minutes	2

Ingredients

- 2 tablespoons butter
- ½ pound ground sirloin
- Salt and pepper to taste
- 1 teaspoon dried parsley
- ½ pound lettuce
- ½ cup chopped walnuts
- ¼ cup grated parmesan cheese
- 1 cup mozzarella balls
- Dressing
- 3 tablespoons olive oil
- 1 tablespoon Dijon mustard
- 3 tablespoons mayonnaise
- 2 tablespoons cream cheese
- Salt and pepper to taste
- 1 teaspoon chili flakes

Directions

Using a nonstick frying pan, heat the oil. Add the ground beef.

Season with salt and pepper and parsley.

Let cool completely.

Put lettuce in a salad bowl and add the cooled ground beef, walnuts, parmesan, and mozzarella balls.

Mix the olive oil, Dijon mustard, mayonnaise, and cream cheese and season with salt and pepper in a jar.

Serve

Nutrition: Calories 340, Fat 20.4, Fiber 6.6, Carbs 22.3, Protein 18.8

Creamy Almond and Ground Beef Salad

Preparation time:	Cooking time:	Servings:
10 minutes	2 hours	2

Ingredients

- 2 tablespoons olive oil
- ½ pound ground sirloin
- Salt and pepper to taste
- 1 teaspoon curry powder
- ½ pound lettuce, chopped
- ¾ cup chopped almonds
- ¼ cup grated parmesan cheese
- 2 hard boiled eggs, chopped
- Dressing
- 3 tablespoons olive oil
- 1 tablespoon Dijon mustard
- 3 tablespoons mayonnaise
- ½ cup cream cheese
- ½ cup sour cream
- Salt and pepper to taste
- 1 teaspoon chili flakes

Directions

Using a nonstick frying pan, heat the butter. Add the ground beef.

Season with salt and pepper and curry powder.

Let cool completely.

Arrange the lettuce in a salad bowl and add the cooled ground beef, almonds, parmesan, and boiled eggs.

Mix the olive oil, Dijon mustard, mayonnaise, cream cheese, and sour cream in a jar and season with salt and pepper and chili flakes.

Serve

Bacon Cheeseburger Balls

Preparation time:	Cooking time:	Servings:
10 minutes	50 minutes	4

Ingredients

- 3 eggs
- 1 envelope onion soup mix
- 1 lb. ground beef
- 2 tablespoons all-purpose flour
- 2 tablespoons whole milk
- 1 cup shredded cheddar cheese
- 4 bacon strips, cooked and crumbled
- 1 cup finely crushed saltine crackers
- 5 tablespoons vegetable oil

Directions

In a mixing bowl, add 1 egg, onion soup mix, and ground beef. Using your hands, mix until well combined. In a small bowl, add the all-purpose flour, milk, cheddar cheese, and bacon. Stir until combined.

Form the cheese and bacon mixture into 36 balls about 1/2" in size. Form the ground beef mixture around the cheese and bacon ball. The meatball should be about 1" in size when finished. In a shallow bowl, add 2 eggs. Whisk until combined. In a small bowl, add the cracker crumbs.

Dip each ball in the eggs allowing the excess liquid to drip off back into the bowl. Roll each ball in the cracker crumbs. You will need to cook the meatballs in two batches.

In a skillet over medium heat, add half the vegetable oil. When it is hot, add half the meatballs. Cook until the meatballs are no longer pink and well browned. Remove the meatballs from the skillet and drain them on paper towels.

Add the remaining vegetable oil and meatballs to the skillet. Cook as directed above. Serve the meatballs hot.

Nutrition: Calories 143, Fat 8.8, Fiber 1.2, Carbs 7.5, Protein 8.8

Enchilada Meatballs

Nutrition: Calories 360, Fat 22.9, Fiber 0.8, Carbs 2.9, Protein 33.6

Preparation time:	Cooking time:	Servings:
10 minutes	30 minutes	4(makes 4 dozen)

Ingredients

- 2 cups crumbled cornbread
- 10 oz. can enchilada sauce
- ½ teaspoon salt
- 1 ½ lbs. ground beef
- 1 ½ cups salsa

Directions

Add the cornbread, enchilada sauce, salt, and ground beef to a mixing bowl. Using your hands, mix until well combined. Form the meat into 1" meatballs. Preheat the oven to 350°. Place the meatballs on a large baking pan.

Bake for 12 minutes or until the meatballs are no longer pink and well browned. Remove the meatballs from the oven and drain the meatballs on paper towels before serving. Place the meatballs in a serving dish. Spoon the salsa over the meatballs and serve.

Bacon Cheeseburger Dip

Preparation time:	Cooking time:	Servings:
10 minutes	30 minutes	4

Ingredients

- 8 bacon slices

- 8 oz. lean ground beef

- 8 oz. cream cheese, cubed

- 2 cups shredded cheddar cheese

- 2 tablespoons chopped fresh parsley

- 10 oz. can of Rotel tomatoes

Directions

Using a nonstick frying pan, heat the butter. Cook the bacon for 8 minutes or until the bacon is done and crispy. Remove the bacon from the skillet and drain it on paper towels.

Add the ground beef to the skillet. Stir frequently to break the ground beef into crumbles as it cooks. Cook for about 8 minutes or until the ground beef is well browned and no longer pink. Drain all the grease from the skillet.

Add the cream cheese, cheddar cheese, parsley, and Rotel tomatoes with juice to the skillet. Stir constantly and cook for 5 minutes or until the cheeses melt.

Crumble the bacon and add to the skillet. Stir until all the ingredients are combined. Remove the skillet from the heat.

Spoon the dip into a serving bowl. Serve with raw vegetables, pita chips, or tortilla chips.

Sweet Ketchup and Bacon Meatloaf

Preparation time:	Cooking time:	Servings:
10 minutes	30 minutes	8

Ingredients

- 2 lbs. lean ground beef

- ½ cup soft breadcrumbs

- ½ cup finely chopped onion

- 2 eggs, beaten

- 2 teaspoons salt

- 1 teaspoon black pepper

- 1 teaspoon dried Italian seasoning

- 4 bacon slices

- ½ cup ketchup

- ½ cup molasses

Directions

Add the ground beef, breadcrumbs, onion, eggs, salt, black pepper, and Italian seasoning to a mixing bowl. Using your hands, mix until well combined.

Line a 15 x 10 x 1 jelly roll pan with aluminum foil. Form the meat into 10 x 4 loaves and place them on the pan.

Preheat the oven to 375°. Bake for 20 minutes. Place the bacon slices over the meatloaf. In a small bowl, add the ketchup and molasses. Stir until well combined. Spread the ketchup mixture over the bacon and meatloaf. Bake for 50 minutes or until the bacon is crispy and the meatloaf is no longer pink and firm. Remove the meatloaf from the oven and cool for 10 minutes before slicing.

Hamburger Broccoli Dip

Preparation time:	Cooking time:	Servings:
10 minutes	30 minutes	8

Ingredients

- 1/2 lb. ground beef

- 1/2 teaspoon salt

- 1 lb. Velveeta cheese, cubed

- 10 oz. can Rotel tomatoes

- 10 oz. pkg. frozen chopped broccoli, cooked

- Corn chips

Directions

Add the ground beef and salt into the pan over medium heat. Stir frequently to break the ground beef into crumbles as it cooks. Cook for about 5 minutes or until the ground beef is well browned and no longer pink. Drain all the grease from the skillet.

Add the Velveeta cheese, Rotel tomatoes, and broccoli to the skillet. Stir constantly and cook until the cheese melts and the dip is thoroughly heated. Remove the skillet from the heat and spoon the dip into a serving bowl. Serve the dip with corn chips.

Family Style Meatloaf with Tomato Gravy

Preparation time:	Cooking time:	Servings:
10 minutes	30 minutes	6

Ingredients

- 1 lb. lean ground beef
- 1/2 lb. lean ground pork
- 1 cup chopped onion
- 1 cup chopped green bell pepper
- 1 egg, beaten
- 1/2 cup cracker crumbs
- 1 tablespoon plus 1 teaspoon chili powder
- ¾ teaspoon salt
- ½ teaspoon black pepper
- 2 tablespoons vegetable oil
- 1 tablespoon all-purpose flour
- 16 oz. diced tomatoes with juice

Directions

Add the ground beef, pork, 1/2 cup onion, 1/2 cup green bell pepper, egg, cracker crumbs, 1 tablespoon chili powder, 1/2 teaspoon salt, and 1/4 teaspoon black pepper to a mixing bowl. Using your hands, mix until well combined. Place the meatloaf in a 9 x 5 loaf pan.

In a skillet over medium heat, add 1/2 cup onion, 1/2 cup green bell pepper, and the vegetable oil. Sauté the vegetables for 5 minutes. Sprinkle the all-purpose flour over the vegetables. Stir until well combined.

Add 1 teaspoon chili powder, 1/4 teaspoon salt, 1/4 teaspoon black pepper, and tomatoes with juice to the skillet. Stir constantly and cook until the gravy comes to a full boil. Remove the skillet from the heat and pour the gravy over the meat in the pan.

Bake for 1 hour or until the ground beef and pork are no longer pink and done. Remove the meatloaf from the oven and cool the meatloaf for 5 minutes before slicing.

Nutrition: Calories 540, Fat 10.5 g, Fiber 9.6 g, Carbs 51.6 g, Protein 11.4 g

Southwestern Classic

Preparation time:	Cooking time:	Servings:
15 minutes	30 minutes	6

Ingredients

- 4 slices bread
- 1 1/4 cups chopped onion
- 1/2 cup chopped green bell pepper
- 1 lb. lean ground beef
- 1/2 lb. lean ground pork
- 2 eggs, beaten
- 10 oz. can Rotel tomatoes
- 3/4 teaspoon salt

Directions

Add the bread to a food processor. Process until you have fine crumbs. Pour the crumbs into a mixing bowl. Add the chopped onion, green bell pepper, ground beef, pork, eggs, Rotel tomatoes with juice and salt to the bowl. Using your hands, mix until well combined. The mixture will not be firm.

Shape the meat into a 12" loaf. Place the loaf on a broiler pan. Preheat the oven to 375°. Loosely cover the meatloaf with aluminum foil. Bake for 1 hour. Remove the aluminum foil and bake for 30 minutes or until the meatloaf is no longer pink, firm, and done. Remove the meatloaf from the oven and cool for 5 minutes before slicing.

Big John's Oyster Motoyaki

Preparation time:	Cooking time:	Servings:
10 minutes	40 minutes	5

Ingredients

- 6 oysters, scrubbed and shucked

- 1 teaspoon butter

- 1/4 cup chopped fresh mushrooms

- 1/4 cup chopped green onion

- 1 cup Japanese mayonnaise (such as Kewpie®)

- 1 tablespoon red miso paste

- 1 teaspoon ground cayenne pepper

- 1 teaspoon ground black pepper

- 1 tablespoon capelin roe (Masago)

- 1 lemon, cut into 6 wedges

Direction

For preheating, set the oven at 400 degrees Fahrenheit or 200 degrees Celsius.

Remove oyster meat from their shells and rinse with cold water, removing any shell fragments or pearl beginnings. Pat them dry with paper towels and cut each into 5 smaller pieces. Rinse the lower half of the shells well, discarding the flat tops.

In a small skillet, melt butter over medium heat and add green onion along with the mushrooms. Cook and stir for 5 minutes until softened.

In a small bowl, whisk together black pepper, cayenne, red miso, and mayonnaise. Spread the mixture into a thin layer on the bottom of each shell.

Divide the oyster meat among the shells and top with mushroom mixture. Thickly cover with the remaining mayonnaise mixture and arrange the shells on a baking sheet.

Bake in a preheated oven on the top rack for 20-25 minutes until the tops turn dark brown.

Garnish with roe and serve the baked oysters with lemon wedges.

Broiled Mochi with Nori Seaweed

Preparation time:	Cooking time:	Servings:
10 minutes	40 minutes	5

Ingredients

- 8 frozen mochi squares

- 1/2 cup soy sauce

- 1 sheet nori (dry seaweed)

Direction

Preheat an oven to 275 degrees C (450 degrees F).

Dunk the mochi into the soy sauce and put it on a baking sheet. Bake for around five minutes or until heated through.

As the mochi cooks, slice dried seaweed into eight strips. Put these strips into a large frying pan on medium heat. Remove them from heat when warmed after about 1 to 2 minutes.

Encase every mochi cake with seaweed and then serve warm.

Cream Cheese and Crab Sushi Rolls

Preparation time:	Cooking time:	Servings:
10 minutes	40 minutes	5

Ingredients

- 1 cup uncooked white rice

- 2 cups water

- 2 tablespoons rice vinegar

- 1 teaspoon salt

- 2 sheets nori seaweed sheets

- 1/4 cucumber, peeled and sliced lengthwise

- 2 pieces imitation crab legs

- 1/2 (3 ounces) package cream cheese, sliced

- 1 teaspoon minced fresh ginger root

Direction

In a saucepan, boil water and rice over high heat. Turn heat to medium-low, place cover, and allow to simmer for 20 to 25 minutes till rice is soft, and the liquid has been soaked in. Mix in salt and rice vinegar. Let cool fully.

Spread out sheets of seaweed. Wet hands with water, then scatter rice equally on every sheet, retaining a half-inch space throughout an edge, lengthwise. In a straight line, set cream cheese, imitation crab meat, and strips of cucumber, across the side opposite of the space. Roll sushi beginning from toppings all the way through the exposed end of the seaweed sheet.

Cut every roll into 5 or 6 portions with a sharp moistened knife. Serve alongside minced ginger.

Chapter 7: Preserves, Spreads, Dips, and Condiments

Moroccan Mezze

Preparation time:	Cooking time:	Servings:
10 minutes	40 minutes	3

Ingredients

- 3 cups Goat Cheese Hummus

- 2 cups Moroccan Spiced Chickpeas

- Extra-virgin olive oil

- 2 teaspoons Moroccan spice blend

- 8 ounces beef jerky (preferably peppered)

- 8 ounces turkey jerky (preferably cured)

- 8 flatbreads

- ½ cup (1 stick) unsalted butter

- 1 garlic clove, finely grated

- ¼ cup chopped fresh parsley

- 16 dates (preferably Medjool)

- You will also need: a large board, a medium bowl, a teaspoon, a small bowl

Directions

Prepare the goat cheese hummus and Moroccan spiced chickpeas according to the recipes. The hummus can be made up to a month ahead of time, but the chickpeas are best served fresh unless you plan to recook them in a pan.

Place the hummus in a bowl and drizzle with extra-virgin olive oil and a sprinkle of the Moroccan spice blend. Put the bowl of hummus in the center of the board with a teaspoon next to it. Place the Moroccan spiced chickpeas in a small bowl above and slightly to the right of the hummus bowl.

Arrange the beef jerky and turkey jerky in the top left corner of the board, and sprinkle them with the remaining spice blend.

Preheat the oven to 350°F. Place the flatbreads on a rimmed baking sheet. In a skillet, melt the butter over high heat. Add the garlic and cook, stirring, for 5 minutes, until the butter has browned slightly. Brush the garlic butter evenly over the flatbreads and evenly sprinkle the chopped parsley on top. Toast in the oven for 7 to 10 minutes, until the edges are golden. Cut into pieces and place them surrounding the hummus bowl.

Place the dates in the bottom right corner.

Drink pairing: Serve with mint green tea and a garnish of fresh mint leaves. Or try a Moroccan spritzer: Combine 1 ounce Cointreau, 1 ounce of gin, and 1 ounce of mandarin liqueur in a cocktail shaker with some ice, shake, and strain into a chilled tall Collins glass. Finish with ginger beer and a garnish of orange slices and mint leaves.

Preparation tip: If you don't have any Moroccan spice mix, a combo of equal parts garlic powder, smoked paprika, and ground cumin will do the trick.

Spanish Seaboard

Preparation time:	Cooking time:	Servings:
10 minutes	40 minutes	3

Ingredients

- 1½ cups Chimichurri

- 12 Roasted Vine Campari Tomatoes

- 1½ pounds Yukon Gold potatoes, quartered

- ¼ cup plus 2 teaspoons of extra-virgin olive oil, divided

- 1 teaspoon sea salt,

- Freshly ground black pepper

- 1 pound octopus tentacles

- ½ cup (1 stick) unsalted butter

- 5 garlic cloves, peeled

- 1 pound of large shrimp, peeled and deveined

- 10 ounces Mahón (or any mild cow milk cheese)

- 1 (12-ounce) jar pickled hot peppers, drained

- You will also need: a large board, a small bowl, a small spoon, a medium bowl, a cheese knife

Instructions

Prepare the chimichurri and roasted tomatoes according to the recipes. The chimichurri can be made up to a week in advance, but the tomatoes are best made fresh and served warm or at room temperature.

Preheat the oven to 375°F.

Place all potatoes on a rimmed baking sheet and drizzle with ¼ cup of olive oil, 1 teaspoon of sea salt, and a few grinds of black pepper. Roast for 40 minutes, until the potatoes are crispy, golden brown, and fork-tender. Place the crispy potatoes in the top right corner area of the board and season with sea salt and pepper.

Preheat a grill or a heavy skillet to high heat. Char the octopus tentacles for 3 to 4 minutes, turning once. Slice into ½-inch pieces and place on the top left side of the board. Drizzle with the remaining 2 tablespoons of olive oil and some sea salt.

Spoon some chimichurri over the octopus. Put the rest in a small bowl with a small spoon, below the octopus.

Heat the butter and garlic in a large skillet over medium-high heat. Sauté the shrimp in the garlic butter, turning once halfway through, until fully pink, about 5 minutes. Use a slotted spoon to transfer the shrimp to a medium bowl and place it in the center of the board.

Place the roasted tomatoes in the bottom left corner.

Place the Mahón cheese in the bottom right area of the board, with a cheese knife.

Place the pickled hot peppers in the middle right area.

Drink pairing: Bodegas Muga Selección Especial Reserva Rioja is a Spanish red wine that complements many varieties of seafood, but especially the octopus and shrimp here. It is berry-scented and barrel-aged, which creates a rich, full-bodied wine that can stand up to the bold flavors of this arrangement.

Preparation tip: To take this spread to the next level, you can braise the octopus in a rich and aromatic broth. In a stockpot, simmer 1 cup (2 sticks) unsalted butter, 4 cups dry white wine, 6 peeled garlic cloves, and 1 cup seafood (or chicken) broth. Place 1 to 2 pounds uncooked octopus tentacles (thawed if frozen) into the stockpot and simmer for 60 to 75 minutes, until firm. Transfer to a colander and let cool for 5 minutes, then peel off the skin by rubbing the tentacles with paper towels. Refrigerate in a covered container for up to 2 days, then char as directed on the day of.

Golden Celebration

Preparation time:	Cooking time:	Servings:
10 minutes	40 minutes	3

Ingredients

- 2 (8-ounce) wheels Camembert

- 1 cup caramel sauce

- 1 cup roasted pecans

- Sea salt

- 5½ ounces truffle salami (we like Creminelli Tartufo Salami), thinly sliced

- 4 Bosc pears, cored and sliced

- 8 fresh figs, cut in half

- 1 pint of fresh white currants (or Rainier cherries)

- 1 chocolate babka

- 1 baguette

- You will need: a large board, a bread knife

Instructions

Preheat the oven to 350°F. Line a rimmed baking sheet with parchment paper and place the two wheels of Camembert cheese on it. Bake for about 20 minutes, until the cheese is soft and melty in the center. Remove and transfer to the center of your serving board.

Gently warm the caramel sauce in a small saucepan just until it's runny, then spoon it over the cheese. Top with a heaping pile of roasted pecans and garnish with a pinch of sea salt.

Place the salami slices near the right bottom of the board.

Arrange the pear slices on the right side of the board, from top to bottom.

Scatter the fig halves around the pears and salami.

Place the white currants above the salami.

Slice half the chocolate babka, and place the slices and the remaining loaf in the top left corner of the board. Place a bread knife next to the loaf.

Tear the baguette into large pieces and place them around the bottom left corner.

Drink pairing: For an equally decadent refreshment, try a soixante-quinze (sometimes called a French 75). This celebratory cocktail pairs beautifully with the caramel, sweet, and nutty notes of the

143

arrangement. Combine 2 ounces of champagne, 1 ounce of gin, ½ ounce of fresh lemon juice, 1 tablespoon simple syrup, and some ice in a shaker. Shake vigorously and strain into an iced champagne glass. Top up with more champagne and garnish with a lemon peel.

Easy Butterscotch Sauce

Preparation time:	Cooking time:	Servings:
10 minutes	40 minutes	3

Ingredients

- ½ cup unsalted butter

- 1 cup packed brown sugar

- 1 cup heavy cream

- About ½ teaspoon regular salt

- About 1 tablespoon vanilla extract

- 2 tablespoons bourbon (optional)

Directions

Place a heavy medium saucepan over medium heat and melt the butter.

Add the sugar and stir. It will be sandy at first, but watch for when the sugar fully dissolves.

When the sugar has dissolved, add the cream and whisk it in. Cook, stirring often until it reaches 225°F.

Remove the pot from the heat and let it cool, and then season with salt and vanilla – be sure to add small amounts and taste it as you go. Add the bourbon, if you're using it.

Pour the sauce into mason jars and cover. Refrigerate.

Hot Fudge Sauce

Preparation time:	Cooking time:	Servings:
10 minutes	10 minutes	3

Ingredients

- 2 cups chocolate chips (your choice, but semi-sweet is what we use)
- ¾ cup granulated sugar
- 1 (12-ounce) can of evaporated milk
- 2 tablespoons unsalted butter
- 1 ½ teaspoons vanilla extract
- ½ teaspoon salt

Directions

Place a heavy saucepan over medium heat and add the chocolate, sugar, evaporated milk, and butter.

Cook for about 5 minutes, or until everything is melted.

Stirring constantly, bring it to a light boil, and remove it from the heat. Stir in the vanilla and salt.

Pour it into mason jars and let it cool, it will thicken.

To reheat, microwave in 30-second intervals.

Rum and Butter Sauce

Preparation time:	Cooking time:	Servings:
10 minutes	10 minutes	3

Ingredients

- ¾ cup unsalted butter

- 1 ½ cups light brown sugar

- ⅔ cup heavy cream

- 6 tablespoons dark rum

- 2 teaspoons vanilla

- Flaked sea salt

- ½ cup sultana raisins (optional)

Directions

Place a skillet over medium heat.

Melt the butter and whisk in the brown sugar until it is well incorporated.

While stirring, drizzle in the cream, rum, and vanilla extract.

Cook, stirring, for about 5 more minutes, and then remove the pan from the heat and let it cool.

Pour it into bottles and seal. Refrigerate for up to 2 weeks.

Vanilla Cream Sauce

Preparation time:	Cooking time:	Servings:
10 minutes	20 minutes	3

Ingredients

- 2 cups heavy cream

- 1 cup granulated sugar

- 2 tablespoons cornstarch

- ½ cup unsalted butter

- 1 ½ teaspoon vanilla extract

- ½ teaspoon salt

Directions

Place a heavy medium saucepan over medium heat and add the cream, sugar, cornstarch, and butter. Mix well and cook until it is bubbly.

Let it boil lightly for about 3 minutes, and then remove it from the heat and add the vanilla and salt.

Pour the sauce into mason jars and let it cool. Refrigerate, and consume within 2 weeks.

Pineapple Ginger Sauce

Preparation time:	Cooking time:	Servings:
10 minutes	40 minutes	3

Ingredients

- 1 cup pineapple juice

- ½ cup orange marmalade

- 1 tablespoon fresh ginger, minced

- 1 tablespoon cornstarch

Directions

Combine all the ingredients in a heavy saucepan over medium heat and cook until bubbly and thick.

Pour the sauce into mason jars and let it cool. Refrigerate, and consume within 3 weeks.

Fireball Whisky Sauce

Preparation time:	Cooking time:	Servings:
7 minutes	15 minutes	3

Ingredients

- 2 cups light brown sugar

- 1 cup butter

- 1 cup heavy cream

- ¾ teaspoon salt

- ½ cup Fireball Cinnamon Whisky

Directions

Combine the sugar, butter, cream, and salt in a saucepan over medium heat. Cook for 5 minutes, until everything is melted together.

Add the whisky and cook for another 10 minutes, until you see the sauce begin to thicken. Get the pot from the heat and let it cool slowly. Pour it into clean jars and seal.

Store in the fridge for up to 2 weeks, if it lasts that long.

An Italian Date

Preparation time:	Cooking time:	Servings:
10 minutes	40 minutes	3

Ingredients

- 5½ ounces speck, thinly sliced
- 10 ounces Salami Picante
- 8 ounces pecorino, sliced
- ¼ cup honey
- 2 (6-ounce) fresh Mozzarella balls
- 2 tablespoons chili oil
- Sea salt
- Freshly ground black pepper
- 1 (12-inch) Neapolitan-style flatbread, pizza crust, or focaccia
- 1½ cups arugula
- Extra-virgin olive oil for drizzling
- You will also need: a large board, a small knife, a small jar or dish, a honey wand or spoon, 2 cheese knives

Directions

Place the sliced speck in the top left area of a large board.

Slice half the Salami Picante and place the slices and remaining large piece in the top center of the board with a small knife, next to the speck.

Place the slices of pecorino below the salami.

Put the honey in a small jar with a honey wand or spoon and place it to the right of the pecorino.

Place the mozzarella balls on the bottom right area of the board. Drizzle the cheese with chili oil and season with sea salt and pepper. Place two cheese knives next to it.

Cut the flatbread into 2-by-5-inch rectangles and layer them to the left of the mozzarella along the bottom of the board.

Drink pairing: Vermentino di Gallura is an Italian white wine made on the island of Sardinia, where the grapes love the sea. This crisp wine has mineral and saline characteristics that bring out the flavors of charcuterie. We also recommend offering a cappuccino or espresso to accompany this board. It is the Italian way, day or night.

A Night In

Preparation time:	Cooking time:	Servings:
10 minutes	40 minutes	3

Ingredients

- 2 cups Pan-Roasted Garlic Almonds
- 4 ounces Jarlsberg
- 4 ounces smoked Gouda
- 4 ounces Dubliner
- 5 ounces salami, thinly sliced
- 5 ounces Tuscan salami, thinly sliced
- 5 ounces spicy salami, thinly sliced
- 1 bunch of red grapes
- 1 bunch green grapes
- 1 pint of raspberries
- 1 cup dried apricots
- 1 traditional baguette, sliced
- 1 sourdough baguette, sliced
- You will need: a large board, 2 cheese knives, a small bowl, a large bowl

Instructions

Prepare the pan-roasted garlic almonds according to the recipe. These can be made up to a week ahead of time.

Cut half of the Jarlsberg wedge into small pieces. Place the rest of the wedge in the top left corner of the board with a cheese knife, and surround it with the smaller pieces.

Place the Gouda in the bottom right area with a cheese knife.

Crumble the Dubliner into bite-size pieces, and pile them in the bottom left area of the board.

Place the slices of regular salami and Tuscan salami above the Gouda, in the middle to the right side of the board. Place the slices of spicy salami in the bottom middle area of the board.

Trim the red and green grapes into small bunches and stack them in the center of the board, creating some height. Cascade some down either side of the board, filling in a few gaps. Sprinkle the raspberries over the grapes.

Tuck the dried apricots into the bottom right corner.

Place a small bowl of almonds on the left side, near some bunches of grapes.

Place a few slices of baguette in any blank spaces, and offer the extra in a large bowl on the side.

Drink pairing: For a fittingly fun beverage, make a caracara mojito, a sweet, citrusy, and herbal cocktail with just the right amount of bubbles. In a tall Collins glass, muddle 1½ ounce white rum, 1 mint sprig, and ½ ounce fresh lime juice. Add 1 ounce of fresh caracara orange juice (or regular orange juice)

Chapter 8: Nuts, Olives, and Pickles

Baked French Brie with Peaches, Pecans, and Honey

Preparation time:	Cooking time:	Servings:
10 minutes	20 minutes	3

Ingredients

- 1 (9") wheel of French Brie
- 1 (15 ounces) can of peaches (cubed)
- ¼ cup pecans (crushed)
- 5 sprigs of fresh thyme
- 3 basil leaves (finely sliced)
- Runny honey (as needed)
- French baguette (sliced, to serve)

Directions

Preheat the main oven to 425 degrees F.

Place the unwrapped Brie in an oven-proof ceramic dish.

Top with the peach cubes.

Scatter the pecans over the top.

Season with thyme and basil, and drizzle over with honey.

Bake in the preheated oven for between 15-20 minutes, or until the cheese is entirely melted and gently browned.

Serve with slices of fresh French baguette.

Cauliflower Pecan Florets

Preparation time:	Cooking time:	Servings:
10 minutes	40 minutes	5

Ingredients

- ¾ cup raw pecan halves

- ¼ cup brown rice flour

- ¾ teaspoon sea salt (divided)

- ½ teaspoon paprika

- ½ teaspoon powdered garlic

- ¼ teaspoon freshly ground black pepper

- ¾ cup water

- 6 cups of cauliflower florets

- Ranch dressing or hot sauce (to serve, optional)

Directions

Preheat the oven to 425 degrees F.

In a food blender or processor, and pulse the pecans to the consistency of flour.

In a bowl, combine the pecan flour with the brown rice flour, ¼ teaspoon of sea salt, paprika, powdered garlic, and freshly ground black pepper.

Pour in the water and mix to a batter-like consistency.

Add the florets to the bowl and toss to evenly coat all over.

Arrange the florets on a baking sheet lined with parchment paper and season with the remaining salt.

Bake in the preheated oven for 15 minutes.

Remove from the oven, flip the florets over, return to the oven, and bake for an additional 10 minutes, until golden brown.

Serve the florets with a side of ranch dressing or your favorite hot sauce.

Cream of Walnut Soup

Preparation time:	Cooking time:	Servings:
10 minutes	60 minutes	3

Ingredients

- 3 cups chicken broth
- 1 cup walnuts (chopped)
- 2 tablespoons of onion (peeled, chopped)
- 2 tablespoons of celery (chopped)
- ⅛ teaspoon ground nutmeg
- 2 tablespoons of butter
- 2 tablespoons of all-purpose flour
- ½ cup 2% milk
- 1 cup half-and-half cream
- Fresh parsley (minced)

Directions

In a pan, combine the broth with the walnuts, onion, celery, and nutmeg and bring to a boil.

Turn the heat down, cover with a lid and simmer for half an hour. Set aside to slightly cool.

Transfer the mixture to a food blender and cover — process to a puree, and strain.

In a large-size pan, over moderate heat, melt the butter.

Stir in the flour until combined.

A little at a time in the milk and bring to boil while cooking and stirring for 60 seconds until thickened. Gradually stir into the puree.

Add the half and half cream, and gently heat.

Garnish with minced parsley and serve.

Feta, Roasted Red Pepper, and Pine Nut Pancakes

Preparation time:	Cooking time:	Servings:
10 minutes	20 minutes	3

Ingredients

- Pancakes

- 1 large-size egg

- 1¾ ounces plain flour

- Pinch of salt

- 3½ ounces milk

- Butter (to fry)

Topping:

- A handful of rocket leaves

- 1 ounce jarred roasted red peppers (drained, cut into thin strips)

- ½ small onion (peeled, thinly sliced)

- 1¾ ounces feta (crumbled)

- 1 ounce of pine nuts (toasted)

- A handful of flat-leaf parsley (coarsely chopped)

- Freshly squeezed juice of ½ lemon

- Salt

- Freshly ground black pepper

Directions

For the pancakes:

Add the eggs, flour, and salt to a bowl, and using a whisk, beat.

Pour in the milk and once again whisk, until silky smooth.

Over moderate heat, melt a knob of butter in a frying pan.

Add the batter to the pan in scoops and cook for 1-2 minutes. Repeat the process for the remaining pancakes.

To prepare the topping:

Scatter a couple of rocket leaves over each of the pancakes. Top with red peppers followed by the onion, feta cheese, and pine nuts.

Garnish with parsley, sprinkle with lemon juice, and season with salt and pepper.

Roll the pancakes up and enjoy.

156

Macadamia Nut Hummus

Preparation time:	Cooking time:	Servings:
10 minutes	10 minutes	3

Ingredients

- 3 cloves garlic

- 2 cups canned chickpeas (drained, liquid reserved)

- 1½ teaspoon salt

- ¼ cup tahini

- 5 tablespoons freshly squeezed lemon juice

- 2 tablespoons chickpea liquid

- ½ cup roasted macadamia nuts

- Olive oil (to drizzle)

Directions

Turn on a food blender and while running, add the garlic via the lid, processing until minced.

Add the chickpeas, salt, tahini, lemon juice, chickpea liquid, and macadamia nuts and blend until smooth.

Drizzle with olive oil, serve, and enjoy.

Pistachio-Crusted Shrimp with Orange Zest

Preparation time:	Cooking time:	Servings:
10 minutes	30 minutes	4

Ingredients

- 20-24 jumbo shrimp (shelled, deveined)
- 1 cup pistachios (coarsely ground)
- 2 small eggs
- 4 tablespoons virgin olive oil
- Sea salt
- Zest of 1 orange

Directions

Pat the shrimp dry with kitchen paper towels.

Add the pistachios to a wide bowl.

Add the eggs to another wide bowl and lightly whisk.

In batches, dip the shrimp in the eggs, shaking off any excess. Cover with the ground pistachios, and again shake off any excess.

Repeat the process until all the shrimp are coated.

Over moderate heat, add the oil to a pan,

Cook the shrimp in the hot oil for 3-4 minutes on each side, or until sufficiently cooked through.

When you are ready to serve, season with salt, sprinkle with orange zest, and enjoy.

Spanish Almond Soup

Preparation time:	Cooking time:	Servings:
10 minutes	2 hours 40 minutes	3

Ingredients

- I cup blanched slivered almonds

- 1 clove of garlic (peeled)

- 2 cups cold filtered water

- 1 cup fresh bread (crusts removed, cubed)

- 1 tablespoon sherry vinegar

- 1 tablespoon extra-virgin olive oil

- Salt and freshly ground pepper (to taste)

- Olive oil (to serve)

- Mint leaves (to serve)

- Toasted almonds (to serve)

Directions

In a food blender, combine the almonds with the garlic and cold water, and process until entirely creamy and smooth.

You need to strain the mixture through a fine-mesh sieve. Start the blender on slow, then move to high speed.

Add the cubes of bread, and once again puree until smooth.

Stir in the sherry vinegar followed by the oil — season with salt and pepper, to taste.

Transfer to an airtight container and place in the fridge, for a minimum of 2 hours.

Stir, drizzle with oil, garnish with mint leaves and toasted almonds and serve, chilled.

Squash and Pecan Flatbread with Ricotta and Dried Cranberries

Preparation time:	Cooking time:	Servings:
10 minutes	40 minutes	3

Ingredients

- 1 delicata squash

- Nonstick cooking spray

- Salt and black pepper

- 4 flatbreads

- ¾ cup ricotta

- ¼ cup dried cranberries

- ½ cup pecan halves

- 2 tablespoons fresh sage (chopped)

Directions

Preheat the main oven to 400 degrees F.

Trim the ends off the delicata squash and slice thinly into rings. Remove the seeds from each ring. Transfer to a baking tray,

Spritz the squash with nonstick cooking spray and season with a pinch each of salt and black pepper.

Place in the oven and bake for 10 minutes, turn over halfway through cooking.

On a second baking sheet, arrange the flatbreads. Top with roasted squash and a large dollop of ricotta cheese. Sprinkle over dried cranberries, pecans, and fresh sage. Season again with salt and black pepper.

Return the flatbreads to the oven and cook for several minutes or until the bread is crisp and golden and the cheese has begun to melt.

Take out of the oven, allow to cool for a couple of minutes, then slice and serve.

Tomato, Raisin, and Pine Nut Bruschetta

Preparation time:	Cooking time:	Servings:
10 minutes	40 minutes	3

Ingredients

- 2 tablespoons extra-virgin olive oil
- 1 large shallot (minced)
- 1 small dried red pepper (seeded, chopped)
- 2 cups cherry tomatoes (washed, cut into quarters)
- Sea salt (to season)
- ½ cup pine nuts
- ½ cup raisins
- 12 (½") slices of ciabatta
- Olive oil (to brush)

Directions

Over moderate-high heat, heat the oil until it begins to ripple.

Add the shallots along with the dried red pepper to the pan, and cook, while frequently stirring until the shallots become transparent.

Next, add the tomatoes followed by a pinch of sea salt.

Reduce the heat to moderate-low and cook for 10-15 minutes, or until the mixture begins to thicken slightly and the tomatoes are a deep orangey-red color. Stir in the pine nuts and raisins.

Cook, while occasionally stirring for an additional 10-15 minutes to allow the raisins to plump and the mixture to thicken.

Season, taste and set aside to slightly cool.

Brush the slices of ciabatta with a drop of olive oil and toast on both sides.

Spread the tomato mixture over the toasted bread and enjoy.

Tropical Chicken Salad

Preparation time:	Cooking time:	Servings:
10 minutes	40 minutes	3

Ingredients

- 2 cups cooked deli chicken (cubed)

- 1 cup celery (trimmed, chopped)

- 1 cup mayonnaise

- ½ - 1 teaspoon curry powder (to taste)

- 1 (20 ounces) can pineapple chunks (drained)

- 2 large-size firm bananas (peeled, sliced)

- 1 (11 ounces) can mandarin orange (drained)

- ½ cup sweetened coconut (shredded)

- Salad greens (optional)

- ¾ cup salted cashews or peanuts

Directions

Add the chicken along with the celery to a bowl.

Add the mayonnaise along with the curry powder (to taste) and mix thoroughly, to combine.

Cover with a lid and chill in the fridge for a minimum of half an hour.

When you are ready to serve, add the pineapple chunks, banana, mandarin orange, and shredded coconut, and gently toss.

Serve on fresh salad greens and garnish with nuts.

Almond Crusted Cheesy Grapes

Preparation time:	Cooking time:	Servings:
10 minutes	20 minutes	3

Ingredients

- 1 cup sliced almonds

- 8 ounces cream cheese (softened)

- 2 ounces blue cheese (room temperature, crumbled)

- 2 tablespoons fresh parsley (minced)

- 2 tablespoons heavy whipping cream (room temperature)

- 1-1¼ pounds seedless red or green grapes (rinsed, patted dry)

Directions

Preheat the main oven to 275 degrees F.

In a food processor, pulse the almonds until finely chopped.

Spread the chopped almonds in a 15x10x1" baking pan and bake for 6-8 minutes, while occasionally stirring until golden.

Transfer the mixture to a shallow bowl and allow it to slightly cool.

In a second bowl, combine the cream cheese with the blue cheese, parsley, and whipping cream until incorporated.

Insert a cocktail stick into each grape.

Roll the grapes in the cheese mixture followed by the almonds.

Arrange the grapes on baking sheets lined with waxed paper.

Transfer to the fridge, covered until you are ready to serve.

Cheddar-Pecan Crisps

Preparation time:	Cooking time:	Servings:
10 minutes	50 minutes	3

Ingredients

- 2 cups unsalted butter (softened)

- 4 cups mature Cheddar cheese (shredded)

- 4 ½ cups all-purpose flour

- 1 teaspoon salt

- ½ teaspoon garlic powder

- ½ teaspoon cayenne pepper

- 1 cup toasted pecans (finely chopped)

Directions

Using a bowl, cream the butter with the Cheddar cheese until fluffy and light.

In a second bowl, whisk the flour with salt, garlic powder, and cayenne pepper. Gradually beat into the creamed butter-cheese mixture.

Fold in the toasted pecans.

Shake the mixture into 8 (10") long logs. Wrap the logs in kitchen wrap and transfer to the fridge for 2 hours, until firm.

Preheat the main oven to 350 degrees F.

Unwrap the logs and cut the dough crosswise into ¼ slices.

Arrange 1" apart on ungreased baking sheets.

Bake in the preheated oven until the edges are lightly browned and crisp, for 12-15 minutes.

Allow to cool on the pan for 60 seconds.

Remove to wire baking racks to cool.

Cook's Note: To toast the pecans, bake while occasionally stirring at 350 degrees F in a shallow pan for 5-10 minutes, until lightly browned.

Curried Tropical Nut Mix

Preparation time:	Cooking time:	Servings:
10 minutes	20 minutes	3

Ingredients

- 2 tablespoons curry powder

- 1 tablespoon butter

- 1 tablespoon olive oil

- ½ teaspoon cayenne pepper

- 1 teaspoon ground cumin

- 6 cups salted, mixed nuts

- 1 cup shredded sweetened coconut

- ½ cup dried mango (chopped)

Directions

In a microwave-safe bowl, combine the curry powder with the butter, olive oil, cayenne pepper, and ground cumin. Uncovered, microwave on high for 30 seconds.

Add the cashews, almonds, peanuts, and shredded coconut; toss to coat evenly.

Cook, uncovered, for an additional 5 minutes until lightly browned, stirring regularly. Add the chopped mangoes.

Spread the mix onto wax paper and set aside to cool. Store in an airtight, resealable container.

Feta-Nut Fritters

Preparation time:	Cooking time:	Servings:
10 minutes	50 minutes	3

Ingredients

- 2.3 ounces short-grain white rice (rinsed and drained)

- ¾ cup water

- Whites of 3 medium eggs

- 12.3 ounces feta cheese (crumbled)

- Salt and black pepper

- 4 teaspoon fresh thyme leaves

- 1 tablespoon hazelnuts (toasted)

- 4 tablespoon fresh breadcrumbs

- 3 tablespoon olive oil

- ½ tablespoon butter

Directions

Add the rice to a saucepan and pour in the water. Bring gradually to a boil, cover, and cook for 20-25 minutes until tender. Take off the heat, do not uncover, and allow to cool.

Whip up the egg whites until they can hold stiff peaks. Fold in the feta and cooled rice.

Season with a pinch each of salt and black pepper. Fold in the thyme.

Shape the mixture into 16 equal balls.

Combine the toasted hazelnuts and breadcrumbs. Roll each ball in this mixture to coat.

In a large pan over moderately high heat, melt together the olive oil and butter. Add the cheese balls to the pan and sauté for a few minutes, frequently turning, until evenly golden.

Remove from the pan, drain on kitchen paper towels, and serve hot.

Macadamia Nut Caramel Popcorn

Preparation time:	Cooking time:	Servings:
10 minutes	40 minutes	3

Ingredients

- 15 cups popped corn

- 2 cups of macadamia nuts (halved)

- 10 tablespoon unsalted butter

- ⅓ cup light corn syrup

- ⅓ cup packed light brown sugar

- ¼ cup granulated sugar

- 1½ teaspoon coarse salt

Directions

Preheat the main oven to 250 degrees F.

Add the popcorn along with the nuts to a large mixing bowl.

Over moderate heat, in a heavy pan, melt the butter.

Stir in the syrup along with the brown sugar, granulated sugar, and ½ teaspoon of coarse salt. Cook until the sugar entirely dissolves, while occasionally stirring.

Increase the heat to high, and bring to boil, without stirring until the temperature registers 248 degrees F on a candy thermometer. It will take between 2-4 minutes to make the caramel.

Pour the caramel evenly over the popcorn mixture, stirring to coat thoroughly.

Transfer the popcorn to 2 rimmed cookie sheets.

Bake in the oven until the coating is hard, for 40-45 minutes, stirring twice. You can test this by taking a few kernels of popcorn out of the oven. If it crisps within 60 seconds of resting at room temperature, it is ready.

Pine Nut and Zucchini Fritters

Preparation time:	Cooking time:	Servings:
10 minutes	40 minutes	3

Ingredients

- ¼ cup pine nuts
- 2 large zucchinis (grated)
- 2 scallions (finely chopped)
- ¼ cup low-fat feta cheese
- 1½ cups wholemeal plain flour
- ¾ cup buttermilk
- 1 medium-size egg (lightly beaten)
- 1 tablespoon flat-leaf parsley (chopped)
- 2 tablespoons sweet chili sauce
- Nonstick cooking spray
- 4 wedges of lemon

Directions

Add the pine nuts, zucchini, scallions, feta cheese, plain flour, buttermilk, egg, parsley, and sweet chili sauce and stir to combine entirely. Set to one side for 10 minutes.

Over moderate heat, heat a frying pan and spritz with nonstick cooking spray.

In tablespoonfuls, add the mixture to the pan and cook for a couple of minutes on each side until cooked through and golden.

Take the fritters out of the pan. Keep warm while you cook the remaining fritter batter.

Garnish with a lemon wedge and serve.

Roasted Almonds with Paprika and Orange

Preparation time:	Cooking time:	Servings:
10 minutes	40 minutes	3

Ingredients

- 1 cup raw whole almonds

- 1 teaspoon extra-virgin olive oil

- ½ teaspoon smoked paprika

- ½ teaspoon flaky sea salt

- Zest of 1 medium orange

Directions

Preheat the main oven to 325 degrees F. Line a baking sheet using parchment paper. Set to one side.

In a mixing bowl, combine the almonds along with the olive oil, smoked paprika, and sea salt.

Spread the mixture evenly over the baking sheet.

Roast in the oven for approximately 15 minutes, stirring every 4-5 minutes until the nuts are golden and fragrant. It is important to make sure the nuts don't burn.

Allow to cool and toss with the orange zest.

Enjoy.

Slow Cooker Candied Nuts

Preparation time: **Cooking time:**   **Servings:**

10 minutes   30 minutes   3

Ingredients

- ½ cup butter (melted)

- ½ cup powdered sugar

- 1 ½ teaspoon ground cinnamon

- ¼ teaspoon ground ginger

- ¼ teaspoon ground allspice

- 1½ cups pecan halves

- 1½ cups walnut halves

- 1 cup unblanched almonds

Directions

In a greased slow cooker of 3-quart capacity, combine the butter with powdered sugar, ground cinnamon, ginger, and allspice.

Add the pecan and walnut halves, tossing to coat evenly.

Cook, while covered on low for between 2-3 hours, until the nuts are crisp. You will need to stir once during cooking.

Transfer the nuts to waxed paper to completely cool.

Honey Mustard Nut Mix

Preparation time:	Cooking time:	Servings:
10 minutes	60 minutes	3

Ingredients

- 2 egg whites
- ¼ cup honey
- 2 tablespoons stone-ground mustard
- 1 tablespoon ground mustard powder
- 1 tablespoon Worcestershire sauce
- 3 cups raw mixed nuts (pistachios, almonds, pecans, and/or walnuts)
- 1 cup large pretzels, roughly chopped
- 1 teaspoon sea salt

Directions

Preheat the oven to 225°F. Line a large baking sheet with foil and butter it generously.

In a mixing bowl, combine the egg whites and beat until they are slightly frothy.

Mix in the honey, mustard, mustard powder, and Worcestershire sauce.

Add the nuts and pretzels and toss to combine.

Spread the mixture on the prepared sheet and bake for 45 minutes to 1 hour, stirring every 15 minutes.

Sprinkle with salt, and let them cool completely before storing in an airtight container.

Candied Pecans

Preparation time: 10 minutes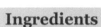

Cooking time: 40 minutes

Servings: 3

Ingredients

- 2 cups granulated sugar
- 1 ½ teaspoon ground cinnamon
- 1 ½ teaspoons salt
- 2 egg whites
- 2 tablespoons water
- 2 pounds pecan halves

Directions

Preheat the oven to 250°F. Line a large baking sheet with foil and butter it generously.

In a small bowl, combine the sugar, cinnamon, and salt. Mix well.

In a large bowl, whisk the egg whites with the water until frothy. Add the pecans and toss, and then stir in the sugar mixture.

Combine everything well and spread it all on the prepared baking sheet.

Bake until golden, about 1 hour, stirring every 15 minutes.

Old South Pralines

Preparation time:	Cooking time:	Servings:
10 minutes	10minutes	3

Ingredients

- 1 cup brown sugar
- 1½ cups white sugar
- ½ cup salted butter
- ½ cup milk or heavy cream
- 1 teaspoon vanilla extract
- ½ teaspoon maple extract
- ½ teaspoon salt
- 1½ cups pecans, chopped

Directions

Line a baking sheet with parchment paper.

In a large saucepan, combine all the ingredients and heat over medium-high heat, stirring frequently until boiling.

Let boil for several minutes, stirring continuously, until temperature registers 240°F on a candy thermometer.

Remove from heat and continue stirring until the mixture begins to thicken and take on a bit of a grainy texture.

Drop dollops of the mixture onto the parchment-lined baking sheets and let cool completely.

Smoky-Sweet Almonds

Preparation time:	Cooking time:	Servings:
10 minutes	30 minutes	3

Ingredients

- ½ cup dark brown sugar

- 2 teaspoons kosher salt

- 1 teaspoon smoked paprika

- ½ teaspoon cayenne pepper

- ½ teaspoon ground black pepper

- 1 large egg white

- 1 ¼ pounds almonds, whole, raw, skin on (about 4 cups)

Directions

Preheat the oven to 300°F. Line a large baking sheet with foil and butter it generously.

In a small bowl, combine the brown sugar, salt, paprika, cayenne, and black pepper.

In a large bowl, whisk the egg white until frothy. Stir in the sugar mixture until well combined, and then toss in the almonds. Stir until they are well coated.

Spread the mixture on the prepared baking sheet and bake for 25 minutes, stirring once.

Let the almonds cool on the tray, stirring and breaking up the clumps from time to time.

Maple Rosemary Nuts

Preparation time:	Cooking time:	Servings:
10 minutes	40 minutes	3

Ingredients

- 2 tablespoons unsalted butter, melted

- 3 tablespoons maple syrup

- ½ teaspoon cayenne pepper

- 1 ½ tablespoon fresh rosemary, finely chopped, divided

- 4 cups nut of your choice (e.g., pine nuts, pecans, walnuts, almonds)

- Sea salt, for sprinkling

Directions

Preheat the oven to 350°F. Line a large baking sheet with foil and butter it generously.

In a mixing bowl, combine the melted butter, maple syrup, cayenne pepper, and 1 tablespoon of the rosemary.

Add the nuts and toss to coat. Spread the nuts on the prepared baking sheet.

Bake for 10 minutes. Stir, and bake for 10 minutes more, watching that they don't burn.

Sprinkle the nuts with the remaining rosemary and salt.

Let them cool completely before storing in an airtight container.

Chocolate Raisin Clusters

Preparation time:	Cooking time:	Servings:
10 minutes	30 minutes	6

Ingredients

- 1 egg white

- ¼ cup sugar

- ¾ cup raisins

- ¾ cup peanuts

- ¾ cup chocolate chips (either milk or semi-sweet according to preferences)

Directions

Preheat the oven to 375°F and place the oven rack in the middle position.

Beat egg white until it becomes frothy.

Add the sugar gradually and continue beating. Stir in the raisins, the peanuts, and the chocolate chips.

Place this mixture in mounds on a cookie sheet lined with a sheet of parchment.

Bake in an oven for 10 minutes.

Let cool completely.

Chocolate Peanut Clusters

Preparation time:	Cooking time:	Servings:
10 minutes	40 minutes	3

Ingredients

- 4 ½ cups peanuts, shelled, salted, unsalted, or dry roasted or a mix

- 1 pound of white chocolate melting wafers

- 10 ounces good-quality semi-sweet chocolate chips

- 8 ounces good-quality milk chocolate, coarsely chopped

Directions

Line 2 baking sheets with parchment paper.

Place the peanuts in a large bowl.

In a metal or heat-proof glass bowl over a pot of lightly simmering water, melt the chocolates, stirring often, until smooth.

Pour chocolate over the peanuts and stir well to coat evenly.

Add spoonsful of the peanut-chocolate mix on the baking sheets.

Refrigerate until set. Store in an airtight container in the refrigerator or arrange in gifting packages.

Keep refrigerated until ready to serve or give.

Fruit and Nut White Clusters

Preparation time:	Cooking time:	Servings:
10 minutes	10 minutes	3

Ingredients

- ½ cup dried cranberries
- ½ cup pumpkin seeds (hulls removed)
- ½ cup sunflower seeds
- ½ cup sliced cashews
- 2 cups good quality white chocolate chips
- ½ teaspoon sea salt

Directions

Prepare a sheet with a layer of foil and spray it lightly with cooking spray.

Combine all the nuts and seeds and set aside ½ cup of the mixture.

In a metal bowl over simmering water, melt the chocolate until smooth.

Add the nuts and fruits (except the ½ cup set aside). Mix quickly to combine.

Spoon out clusters of the chocolate-covered nuts onto the prepared pan. Before they set, sprinkle with salt and top with a few of the reserved nuts and berries.

Swedish Nuts

Preparation time:	Cooking time:	Servings:
10 minutes	40 minutes	5

Ingredients

- ½ cup butter
- 2 egg whites
- 1 cup sugar
- 3-4 cups raw pecans

Directions

Preheat the oven to 350 degrees F.

Add the butter to a 9x13" pan and melt in the oven.

Beat the egg whites until stiff.

Add the sugar to the egg whites and continue beating.

Fold the nuts into the egg white-sugar mixture and spread into the baking pan.

Bake the pecans in the oven for between 30-40 minutes, stirring after the first 8-10 minutes. Continue to stir every 4-5 minutes, until done.

Set aside to cool.

In the meantime, and while the pecans cool, you will need to keep stirring.

Trail Mix with Dark Chocolate and Toasted Coconut

Preparation time:	Cooking time:	Servings:
10 minutes	40 minutes	3

Ingredients

- 1 cup unsweetened coconut flakes

- 1 cup raw almonds

- 1 cup raw walnuts

- 1 cup lightly salted, roasted cashews

- ½ cup raw sunflower seeds

- 1 cup dried cherries

- ¾ cup dark chocolate chunks

Directions

Add the coconut flakes to a small frying pan on the stove and over moderate-low heat, while frequently stirring, toast until fragrant and lightly golden. This will take 2-3 minutes. Take care not to allow the mixture to cool.

Add the toasted coconut along with the almonds, walnuts, cashews, sunflower seeds, cherries, and dark chocolate chips to a large mixing bowl, stir to combine.

Store in a resealable container.

Baked Cod with Walnuts

Preparation time:	Cooking time:	Servings:
10 minutes	40 minutes	5

Ingredients

- 4 (5 ounces) cod fillet (rinsed, patted dry)
- Salt and freshly ground black pepper
- Fresh lemon juice
- 2 red onions (peeled, chopped)
- 2 garlic cloves (peeled, finely chopped)
- 1 zucchini (sliced)
- 1 red pepper (diced)
- 1 green bell pepper (seeded, diced)
- 1 cup yellow cherry tomatoes
- 5 tablespoons olive oil (divided)
- 2 tablespoons cracked rosemary needles
- ½ cup walnuts (shelled)

Directions

Preheat the oven to 400 degrees F.

Season the cod with salt and black pepper. Drizzle fresh lemon juice over the top.

Add the onion, garlic, zucchini, red pepper, green pepper, tomatoes to an oven-safe dish and season.

Drizzle 4 tablespoons of olive oil over the veggies and sprinkle over the rosemary.

Arrange the fish on top of the veggies and bake in the oven for between 15-20 minutes.

When only 5 minutes of cooking remains, remove the fish from the oven, scatter with walnuts, and return to the oven.

Enjoy.

Cashew Nut and Pesto Pasta

Preparation time:	Cooking time:	Servings:
10 minutes	20 minutes	3

Ingredients

- 7 ounces fusilli pasta
- 10 Cashew nuts
- 2 garlic cloves (peeled)
- Sea salt and freshly ground black pepper
- squeezed juice of 1 lemon
- 2 handfuls of rocket leaves (washed, dried, chopped)
- Olive oil
- 2 tablespoons Parmesan cheese (freshly grated)
- A handful of basil leaves (chopped)

Directions

Cook the pasta according to the package directions and until al dente. Drain and keep warm.

Meanwhile, add the nuts to a pestle and mortar and pound to form a coarse powder.

Next, add the garlic along with a pinch of sea salt, and once again, pound.

Add the lemon zest and juice to the mixture and continue to pound and mash to a pesto-like consistency.

Add enough oil to create a sauce and stir in the grated Parmesan.

Season with more salt and black pepper and stir through the warm pasta.

Cashew, Spinach, and Cannellini Bean Stew

Preparation time:	Cooking time:	Servings:
10 minutes	20 minutes	3

Ingredients

- 2 tablespoon olive oil (divided)

- 17 ounces spinach (washed, dried, chopped)

- 24 ounces tomato passata

- 1 cup cashew butter

- 2 (14 ounces) cans of cannellini beans

- 1 teaspoon each of salt and freshly ground black pepper (to taste)

- 2 teaspoons curry powder

- Pinch of cardamom (to taste)

- A handful of cashew nuts

- 1 teaspoon salt

- Scallions (to serve)

Directions

Heat 1 tablespoon of oil in a large pan.

Add the chopped spinach to the pan and fry for between 2-3 minutes.

Next, add the passata along with the cashew butter, mix well to combine. Heat on moderate heat to a near boil.

Add the beans to the pan and season to taste with salt, black pepper, and 1 teaspoon curry powder. Add a pinch of cardamom and keep heated but do not allow it to boil.

In a small-size pan, heat the remaining oil.

Add the cashews along with the salt and remaining 1 teaspoon curry powder. Stir to combine and roast for a few minutes to allow the nuts to lightly brown. Remove from the heat.

Transfer a large portion of the stew to a serving bowl, scatter with cashews, and garnish with scallions.

Enjoy.

Chargrilled Lamb Cutlets with Macadamia Pesto

Preparation time:	Cooking time:	Servings:
10 minutes	40 minutes	3

Ingredients

3 cups packed fresh basil leaves

½ cup extra virgin olive oil (divided)

1 tablespoon freshly squeezed lemon juice

¼ cup raw macadamia nuts

1 large clove of garlic (peeled, crushed)

Pinch of salt

12 lamb cutlets

Directions

In a blender, process the basil leaves along with ¼ cup of oil until finely chopped.

Add the freshly squeezed lemon juice followed by the macadamia nuts, garlic, salt, and remaining olive oil, and process until smooth.

Add a drop more oil if needed, and season to taste.

Grill the lamb cutlets for 3-4 minutes on each side, or to your preferred doneness.

Remove the lamb cutlets from the grill and serve with the pesto.

Creamy Cashew Curry

Preparation time:	Cooking time:	Servings:
10 minutes	40 minutes	3

Ingredients

- 10 ounces raw cashews
- 1 teaspoon salt
- 1-2 tablespoon coconut oil
- ½ medium-size onion (peeled, chopped)
- 2 bay or curry leaves
- 2 teaspoons Sri Lankan curry powder
- ¼ teaspoon turmeric powder
- ½ teaspoon cayenne pepper
- ½ teaspoon sugar
- 1½ cups premium quality coconut milk
- 1 cup of frozen peas
- Salt (to season)

Directions

Add the cashews to a mixing bowl, and add sufficient room temperature, to cover.

Add 1 teaspoon of salt and mix well to dissolve. Cover the bowl and set it aside to soak for 8-24 hours.

When you are ready to begin cooking, drain the cashews, and set them to one side.

Over moderate heat, eat approximately 1-2 tablespoons of coconut oil.

Add the onions and sauté until translucent.

Next, add the curry or bay leaves and sauté for 3 minutes, or until fragrant.

Stir in the cashews along with the curry powder, turmeric, cayenne, sugar, a pinch of salt, and coconut milk. Mix to incorporate.

Cover and simmer for 45 minutes. Make sure to check from time to time to ensure that there is sufficient liquid in the pan. Add additional water if necessary. Taste and season with salt, if needed.

The cashews are ready when they are al dente.

Add the peas along with additional water if the gravy appears too thick.

Cook until the peas are heated and cooked through and the gravy simmer, for approximately 10 minutes.

Serve with rice and enjoy.

Conclusion

In some regions, charcuterie includes preserving fish using similar methods, to produce delicacies such as smoked salmon, lox, and pickled herring.

In today's world, the term has come to mean pairing preserved meats or seafood with cheeses, fruits, and many other accompaniments to serve at gatherings and celebrations. During get-togethers in our own home, charcuterie spreads serve as a focal point for family and friends to socialize and enjoy an abundance of flavors and textures from all over the world.

Charcuterie boards are not only gorgeous they contain a combination of flavor and nibbles for a simple no-fuss party snack

It's not difficult to prepare a cheese and meat board that everyone will rave about. Adding simple flavors from simple everyday ingredients takes very little prep and just a minute to build.

Made in United States
Troutdale, OR
11/29/2023

15045749R00111